THE MOUNT WHITNEY GUIDE:

30 Years on The Mountain

Whitney Portal Store, remodeled 1997

The Mount Whitney Guide

30 YEARS ON THE MOUNTAIN

A COMPREHENSIVE TRAIL GUIDE

Formerly Published as:

MOUNT WHITNEY:
Mountain Lore from the Whitney Store

Doug Thompson
with
Elisabeth Newbold

Third Edition, Revised

Westwind Publishing Company, El Cajon, California

THE MOUNT WHITNEY GUIDE:
30 Years on The Mountain:

A COMPREHENSIVE TRAIL GUIDE

Formerly Published as:

Mount Whitney:
Mountain Lore from the Whitney Store

by Doug Thompson
with Elisabeth Newbold

Published by:
Westwind Publishing Company
548 N. Westwind Drive
El Cajon, CA 92020

All rights reserved. No part of this book may be reproduced or transmitted in any form or by any means, electronic or mechanical, including photocopying, recording or by any information storage and retrieval system without written permission from the authors, except for the inclusion of brief quotations in a review.

Copyright © 1997, 2003, 2019
by Doug Thompson with Elisabeth Newbold
First Printing 1997
Second Printing 2002, completely revised
Third Printing, 2019, enhanced
PRINTED IN THE UNITED STATES OF AMERICA

Library of Congress Cataloging-in-Publication Data
Doug Thompson with Elisabeth Newbold
    The Mount Whitney Guide: 30 Years on The Mountain by Doug Thompson with Elisabeth Newbold. – 3rd ed.
  p. cm.
  ISBN 978-0-9653596-9-6
  1. Mt. Whitney (Calif.)—Guidebooks. 2. Backpacking—California. 3. Hiking—California. 4. Sierra Nevada—Guidebooks. I. Title

Library of Congress Catalog Card Number: 2018914219

All photos © Jeff Mahoney unless otherwise noted.

Dedication

This book is another step in the passage along the Road of Life. It would not have been possible without all the people, places, and things we have experienced and stored up in our minds for some future time when the rivers run a little slower and grass is a little shorter.

The least important input into the making of the material was myself. The pieces of the picture come from the mountains, and from the time spent with so many people we have come to know. On trips into the many canyons and ridges, it is the exchange of humanness that happens when you share a hike or walk with someone who also understands that it is the flowers, trees, rocks and rivers, birds, bears, and the quietness of the desert that are the true success stories in our lifetime.

When we started to run the Store, we knew we would be tested on many fronts. We approached this adventure with the idea that we would try to adjust to the various demands as they arose. Even our wildest dreams could not come close to what we have experienced and learned since.

Nature has a very distinct cycle—we just don't know what it is. Once we accepted that bit of wisdom, knowing that today will only be like today once, we came to learn that in the morning new things will start and begin another today. Sometimes the experience will be snow, or sometimes bees, butterflies, ladybugs, ants or bears, waterfalls roaring or moon shining on the majestic walls that surround us. This is what we can dedicate a portion of this work to—our growing.

The most important people of my life are my family: my wife, son, daughter-in-law, grandchildren, brothers, mother, and their families; and my wife's family that came to this country from another, seeking all its hope and glory. What we have gained in our mountain experience has, at times, taken us apart from our family ties. I hope this will be recognized as a greater need, to be fulfilled with greater joy.

It would not be possible to close without a confession of my belief that we are passing through here as everyone else—no stronger, no braver, no wiser—just a little luckier that our stay will be a little longer.

To my wife, for the many nights she has been so tired that she couldn't sleep; and my son, who has grown into a man on this mountain, coming to understand his own self and nature. As a family, Mom, Pop, Son, Daughter-in-Law, and grandkids, we hope we can flip a few more burgers, cook a few more hotcakes, take a few more walks, answer a few more questions, and help out on a few more rescues.

Thank you,
Doug Thompson

To my late Father, Eugene B. Barnes, Jr., in appreciation of his lifelong gifts to me: a love of walking in mountains among wild things, and a propensity for working with words.

To my husband, Max Newbold, in gratitude for his vision of this book, and his support in bringing it to fruition.

Elisabeth Newbold

Acknowledgments

The authors are grateful to the many people who helped in the writing and publication of this book. We gathered information and photographs from many sources, and appreciate all those who contributed, as follows:

- All visitors who signed the Guest Book and message board for your "quotable quotes" sprinkled throughout
- George Marsh for material and photos on Gustave Marsh
- Tom LaRocca for his personal account of climbing Mt. Whitney
- County of Inyo, Eastern California Museum for historical photos
- Marcyn Del Clements for lists of flowers and birds, and a poem
- Kayla Browne, Maura Perez, Tamra Riesen, Russell Simon, Julissa Villalobos, and Nayeli Villalobos for proofing
- Jessica Royale Dews for transcribing and proofing
- Earlene and Doug Thompson, Jr. for their recipes, ideas, patience, and tolerance of all the interruptions this book's writing caused in their lives
- Max Newbold for his many good ideas and never-ending faith in us
- Shawn Trueman for help with the weather chapter
- Gilda Garcia, Marc Moreau, Shin Namura, Corinne Newton, Jack & Betsy Northam, Richard Piotrowski and Bob Rockwell for photos
- Rochelle Keene for Big-One-In-One-Day testimonial
- Jeff Mahoney for photos, design, layout and editing

CONTENTS

INTRODUCTION .... **XVII**
   Introduction to First Edition xvii
   Updated Introduction to Second Edition xx
   Introduction to Third Edition xxiii

1. CLIMBING THE MOUNTAIN **1**
   THE BIG ONE IN ONE DAY 17
   TRAIL GUIDE 31
      Trailhead: Mile 0.0, 8,367' 31
      Carillon Drainage: Mile 0.5 32
      First Serious Stream Crossing: Mile 0.65 32
      Entrance to John Muir Wilderness: Mile 0.85, 8,480' 32
      Lone Pine Lake: Mile 2.8, 9,420' 34
      Big Horn Sheep Park: Mile 3.5 34
      Outpost Camp: Mile 3.8, 10,360' 35
      Mirror Lake: 4.3 mi., 10,640' 35
      Trailside Meadow: 5.3 mi., 11,395' 36
      Consultation Lake: 5.8 mi. 37
      Trail Camp: 6.3 mi., 12,039' 37
      Switchbacks: 6.5-8.5 mi., 12,039-13,777' 38
      Trail Crest: 8.5 mi., 13,645' 39
      John Muir Trail Junction: 9.0 miles, 13,480' 40
      Summit: 11 miles, 14,508' more or less. 42
      Going Down 42
      Trailhead: 22 miles, 8,367' 46
   THE MOUNTAINEER'S ROUTE 49
      Why You Shouldn't Go If You Aren't Ready 49
      Description 51
   WHEN SOMETHING GOES WRONG 57
      The Saturday Night Special 58
      Rescues 60
      What Happens at The Store 62
   THE BEARS 67
   THE WILDLIFE 73
   WEATHER 77
   YOUR SUCCESS FACTORS 83
      Your Mental and Physical Preparation 86
      How Long Will It Take? 89

CONTENTS

THE GEAR THING 91
    Packs 95
    Luxury items, Non-luxury items, and Food 96
MOONLIGHT HIKING 98
THE FOUR ZONES 101
CELL PHONES 106
UNPLANNED ACTS 107
    Slips and Falls 109
NOW THE PHYSIOLOGY: Hippos or Hypos? 117
WATER STOPS 120
    Quick list of some often-quoted information 122
    Some Hints 124
WINTER 127

2. MORE INFORMATION 131
LIFE AT THE TOP 131
    Celebrations 131
    The Hut...132
    Sleeping on the Summit 134
RETURN VISITS 151
SPECIAL OCCASIONS 155
OTHER APPROACHES AND LOCAL TRAILS 159
THE MOUNTAIN 167
    Elevation of Mt. Whitney...168
THE PORTAL 171
THE STORE 175
RECIPES FROM THE WHITNEY PORTAL KITCHEN........181
A BRIEF HISTORY 187
    First Ascents and Place Names.....................................187
    Who Built the Trail, and When? 189

BIBLIOGRAPHY 203
Appendix A: This Year or Never 206
Appendix B: The Highest House in America 215
Appendix C: Observations of Halley's Comet 224
Appendix D: Lists Of Flowers and Birds.................................227
Appendix E: Celebrating Mt. Whitney.....................................236
Appendix F: Timeless Mountain 240

A monsoonal morning view of Mt. Whitney

WARNING
DISCLAIMER

This book was written to provide information for those interested in the subject matter covered. It is offered with the understanding that neither the authors nor the publisher are engaged in providing professional guidance for wilderness hikers or climbers. If expert assistance is required, the services of a competent guide should be sought.

It is not the purpose of this book to reprint all information available to the author and/or publisher. A compilation of all the material in print would fill several volumes and exceed the scope of this work. Our intent is to supplement other sources, sharing our unique perspective of this remarkable refuge. We urge you to read all the material available, learn as much as you can about Mount Whitney, and tailor the information to your individual needs. For more information, see the references in the Bibliography.

Every effort has been made to include information that is as accurate and up-to-date as possible. However, there may be errors both typographical and in content. Therefore, this book should be used only as a general guide and not as the ultimate source on this subject. Furthermore, the text contains information only as current as the printing date.

The purpose of this volume is to educate and entertain. The authors and Westwind Publishing shall have neither liability nor responsibility to any person or entity with respect to any loss or damage caused, or alleged to be caused, directly or indirectly by the information contained in this book.

If you do not wish to be bound by the above, you may return this book to the publisher for a full refund.

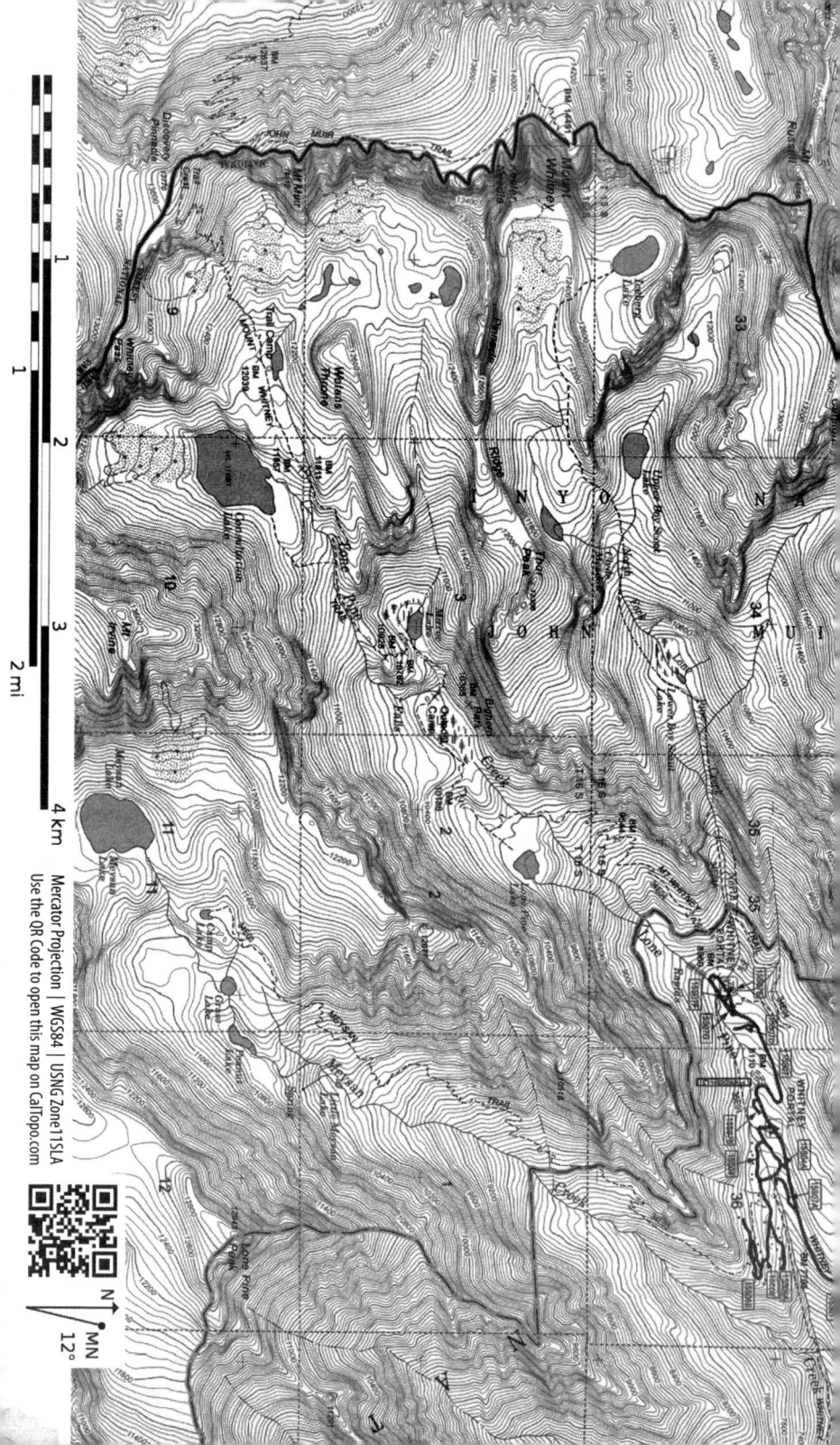

MT. WHITNEY
USC & GS EL= 14,494.164

FIRST ASCENT: August 18, 1873, C. Begole, J. Lucas, A. Johnson

FIRST TRAIL: built in 1904 by local residents. The hut on the summit was built by locals in 1909 for scientists. The trail was rebuilt/re-routed several times and pack animals would take people to the summit. Pack animals are no longer allowed on the trail and the first part of the trail, which was steep, was changed to the present location.

TRAIL MILEAGE AND ELEVATIONS:

	MILES	KM	FEET	METERS
WHITNEY PORTAL TRAIL HEAD	0	0	8,360	2,548
JOHN MUIR WILDERNESS SIGN	0.5	0.8	8,500	2,591
LONE PINE LAKE	2.5	4.0	9,850	3,002
OUTPOST CAMP	3.5	5.6	10,365	3,159
MIRROR LAKE	4.0	6.4	10,640	3,243
TRAILSIDE MEADOW	5.0	8.1	11,395	3,473
TRAIL CAMP	6.0	9.6	12,000	3,658
TRAIL CREST	8.2	13.2	13,777	4,199
JOHN MUIR TRAIL	8.7	14.0	13,480	4,109
MT. MUIR	9.0	14.5	14,015	4,272
KEELER NEEDLE	10.2	16.4	14,000	4,267
MT. WHITNEY SUMMIT	10.7	17.22	14,494	4,417

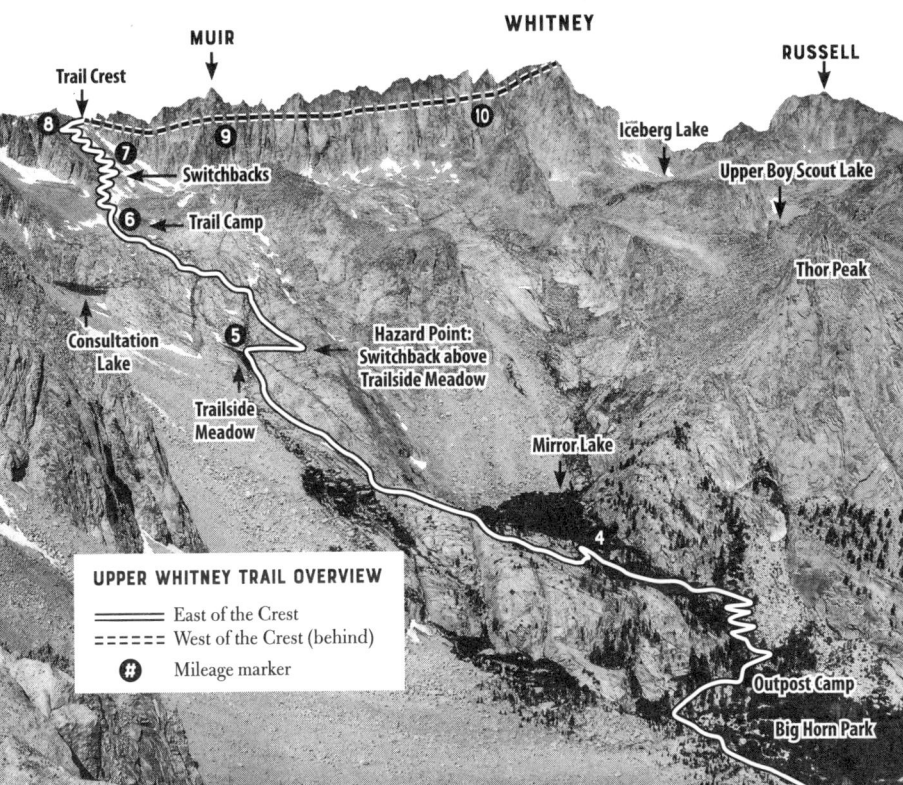

Doug & Earlene Thompson
at the Whitney Portal Store
(photo by Corinne Newton)

INTRODUCTION

Introduction to First Edition

If you're about to climb the Whitney Trail, whether it's for the first time or the hundredth, you naturally have questions about weather, trail conditions, and how late the store is open. If you've just come down from the mountain, you bring back answers to these questions and more. You also want to talk to some fellow human beings and share your experience with people who appreciate it. For this reason, the Whitney Store has become a place of lively conversation.

The Store is owned by Doug and Earlene Thompson, their son, Doug Jr. and daughter-in-law Becky. All four are gracious hosts, good listeners, and great story-tellers. This makes the atmosphere one of friendly camaraderie.

Mt. Whitney stories are served up with breakfast, lunch, and dinner, if you want to listen. But most people would rather talk, and they do. The societal barriers we keep around us for protection in our everyday lives are lowered in this place. The Mountain reminds us of our insignificance, and our brotherhood. Visitors realize more clearly how dependent they are upon each other, and strangers become friends easily and quickly.

Several books have already been written about Mt. Whitney. This mountain's story is a tale full of geological terms, botanical descriptions, historical accounts, and environmental concerns. Personally, we think everyone who has ever climbed Mt. Whitney could write a book about his or her own experience. Each book would be unique because each one's time on the mountain is a reflection of who this person really is.

This is not just another book about Mt. Whitney. It is also a book about you—people who are drawn to The Mountain for one reason or another. People come here from all parts of the world. Each one carries a unique set of expectations, led here by his or her own particular motivation. Almost everyone visits the Whitney Portal Store, a little country kitchen affair offering hot food, hot showers, hiking supplies, and souvenir T-shirts. The friendly folks who run the store have seen and heard it all—dumb questions, outlandish outfits, family arguments, life-threatening situations, life-changing events, and heart-warming heroics.

The humor, pathos, and drama of being human is evident in the microcosm of the Whitney Store. Visitors have left their impressions in the Guest Book and in the minds of the storekeepers. These tales are passed across the counter, free of charge, by the Thompsons. The Whitney Store offers more than money can buy.

This book is a collection of information related to Mt. Whitney and the surrounding area. In response to the huge volume of questions asked about the Whitney Trail, the "Store People" made up a few handouts with vital information about the area. These pages were the seeds that grew into this book, where you will find valuable insights gained through years spent at the Whitney Store, the most detailed trail guide ever published, and a brief history of the area.

We have also included recipes for popular menu items served at the Store over the years. All this is intermingled with selected quotes from the Guest Book, previously unpublished photos, and stories of peoples' unique and interesting experiences. If you've been here before, perhaps you'll recognize your Guest Book entry or your own special story.

Many volumes of information were consulted during the research for this book. One of the more difficult tasks in putting it together was not so much deciding what to include, but what to omit. We want to emphasize that this book is not intended to be a conclusive work. Its purpose is to offer a unique perspective of Mt. Whitney. It springs from a desire to share our experiences, and to help others discover their own.

Meeting our many visitors from around the world has convinced us that we all share a common need to return to nature. The Mt. Whitney area attracts people from all walks of life. Some bring a desire to conquer the mountain; some come just to experience it. Individual fulfillment can be found either way. Those who approach the mountain as an obstruction to be defeated are usually turned back by natural forces or their inability to adjust to them. We cannot control nature. Success comes by embracing it and letting our bodies adapt to it.

We have included a selection entitled "This Year or Never" in Appendix A describing one hiker's Mt. Whitney climb. This piece offers a fairly typical experience of one individual who set a personal goal and was able to reach it. The account is representative of how men and women respond as they pass through this area on their "Road of Life."

Some hikers come here with a lifetime of mountaineering experience, and some with absolutely none. Hopefully, this trail can be an introduction to how people can, by their own acts, enrich or destroy their own lives as well as the fragile environment. We are certain it is only the people who come to this mountain, and the choices they make, that control the impact on its ecology. It is not so much a factor of the number of people who visit Mt. Whitney, but of what those people do when they get here.

We hope you enjoy this book. Please stop by the Store and let us know how you liked it.

Whitney Portal Store
Operated under Permit from Inyo National Forest Service
P.O. Box 61, Lone Pine, CA 93545
For questions or comments please give us a call at:
Whitney Portal Hostel (760) 876-0030

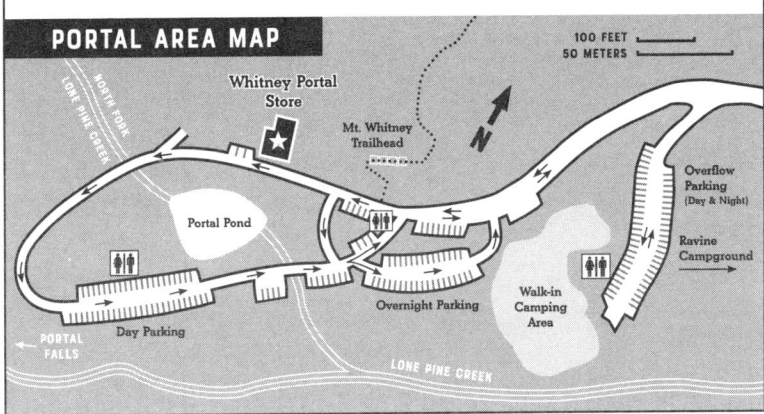

Updated Introduction to Second Edition

The time has come to print the second edition of the Mount Whitney Guidebook. We welcome the opportunity for correcting and editing names and updating information. We've added new photos and quotes. Also, the reality that the reservation system will never stay the same has directed us to write that section with a new perspective. Included here are some thoughts and observations we've made over the past five years since the first edition was published.

We now realize there is a critical lack of information on campgrounds. Data is available, but the challenge is finding it for all the campsites—federal, state, county, and private. It is also vital to know which places are available for advance reservation and which are open on a walk-in basis the day you arrive. (See FAQ #15, p. 10.)

Major improvements were made on the Whitney Trail during the 1998, 1999, and 2000 seasons. Large sections were reworked to repair snow and ice damage above Trail Camp, and erosion control and tread damage all the way down to the trailhead. A great job was done by the trail crews. A great deal of effort is needed to maintain the section from Trail Crest to the summit. With winter conditions for ten months a year, snow and ice damage requires almost constant trail repair and clearing. The last 400 feet of elevation gain and half mile of trail can be impossible to follow due to the many false trails and the snow that stands in the saddle around Keeler Needle. Trail work is ongoing, and the cable area took a major hit during the snow event in 2016, causing the poles to lean beyond use for support. Work to rebuild the trail from Keeler Needle to summit was completed but rock/snow can cover short sections and a direct path is established by hikers each year.

Bears, Bears, Bears! Food, Food, Food! Cars, Trucks, Vans! Incidents of bears breaking into vehicles have increased to the point where new restrictions are now in effect in the Whitney area. You MUST use a bear canister while on the Whitney Trail overnight.

Do NOT leave food in your car while at the Portal—store it in a bear locker. We've added a new chapter devoted entirely to the bears.

We'd like to remind you to take your keys when you leave your car parked at the Portal, and give a spare key to someone in your group. We see people who purposely lock their keys in the car so they won't have to carry them on the trail. They expect to call AAA to get help. This is the wilderness, and you left those conveniences behind when you left the city. Remember that special security system you bought? Now you are the thief, trying to break into your vehicle.

AAA is not quick! It may take 4-6 hours. When you call for service your cell phone kicks out a geographical location (lat/long) of Visalia, which would be the closest office (air distance) so if you need service, make sure you explain this to the DISPATCHER!! Next, when asked for the address, you are "13 miles west of Lone Pine at the end of Whitney Portal Road." Just getting them to understand that will take about an hour.

There is not a local locksmith in Lone Pine. Because of the new chip keys and electronic locks, most cars will need to be towed to a dealer 100-200 miles away, or a replacement key will need to be shipped/driven to the area. There is no Postal Service at the Portal, and the Post Office in Lone Pine is closed on Saturdays and Sundays. FedEx or UPS are your best option. Now where to ship: to your hotel or to us? Our address in town is Whitney Portal Hostel & Hotel, 238 South Main Street, Lone Pine, CA 93545. You may get lucky and use our other address: Whitney Portal Store, 13 Miles West of Lone Pine, CA 93545. UPS and FedEx may come up. If busy, UPS will drop off at The Hostel. GET IT?? Bring an extra key, or make sure it is safely secured in your pack. Oh, and don't lock the pack in the trunk till you grab the key. Coming into the Store and saying, "I have AAA" won't impress the cook or bottle washers. Another hint: purchase the 200-mile tow coverage. The recent season tow/mileage price was quoted $8.00/mile.

Our website, www.mountwhitneyportal.com, has a message board where you should be able to review the postings and glean a wide view of the "Whitney experience." Visitors range from first-time hikers to someone who has hiked the Whitney Trail for over 50 years, with close to 100 summits to pull from. Look at the photos, read the trip reports, enjoy the stories of bears and marmots, study the trail conditions, and the reasons why they summited or didn't.

We cover the trail in one separate chapter, and the one-day hike in another. Your success in reaching the summit is largely determined by the first step you take the day you start planning your trip. You are building the foundation of your journey. Stair steppers, treadmills, and gyms are good, and can condition you somewhat, but you need to build your long-term endurance. How? Stay on your feet actively for 10-12 hours. Experience the outdoors—wind, sun, rain and snow, and uneven ground. Sense how you process food and water, what body parts rub together, what small efforts you can take to reduce potential discomfort, and how you react to these discomforts.

Every time it rains, snows, or blows, the store fills with people worried about the weather. We came up with a universal weather report: "If you have to ask, you are probably not ready to go." I walked up to the Portal one winter's day in deep snow and high wind. I checked the store for damage and noticed a tent by the old trailhead. I thought maybe someone was in trouble and went to check. I found a young man sitting on a rock drinking tea and eating raisins. We talked for hours, sharing tea and snacks. I walked home that night in the dark. We both understood the weather—he a doctor from Russia, and me a kid from Kansas and Colorado. We had many stories to share about cold and growing up playing outdoors in frozen clothes—the tingling and itching at night by the stove. Your concept of beauty is based on your file cabinet.

—**Doug Thompson,** April 2002, updated August 2018

Introduction to Third Edition

"Two county fairs and a hog calling, really?! Now you are qualified to write a book on Whitney?!" Well, no, just a re-write of the first and second edition. And a look back over the last 30 years at the Store, and reflections on some of the early hikes and climbs (1968 or was it 1973?).

Anyway, here's my story, and I'm sticking to it. I never gave it much thought about our background, I just assumed we were average folks. I left home at 10 years old and made it to about the 8th grade in school. Did odd jobs: farm work, construction, plumber's helper, upholsterer, climber, pot and pan dishwasher; cut carnations, cut Christmas trees for two seasons in Colorado, sold fruit along the road in Wyoming, and won $10.00 steer wrestling in Kansas. In 1961 we wrecked our truck in Alabama. We were run off the road early in the morning by a car playing chicken. On the east side of town another vehicle was run off the road, killing 4 young men. I got 330 stitches and took the train back to Denver. My stepdad stayed. He had serious injuries and was not released for quite some time. I decided to fight the commies in Cuba on November 6, 1962. When I walked in to sign up, they told me, "We have a test you won't pass." Well, the U.S. Coast Guard must have needed bodies. After boot camp I was transferred to Long Beach, CA. I thought I would be on a little boat, cruise the harbor, and work on diesel engines. I was placed on a big boat that had boilers, and spent many months at sea from La Paz, Mexico to Attu, Alaska.

We sailed from Long Beach to Hawaii to Japan; I was on the same ship that did the only mid-Pacific rescue for a commercial flight from San Francisco to Hawaii back in 1953. We looked for missing boats, ran aground at a famous yacht race, and launched small boats into the breakwater. I am sure we did some great things, but being a boiler tender, not much happened from my view, except we worked 12-hour days watching the smokestack and water column. I was able to help many young people pass exams and get on-the-job training. I also served as shore patrol in several ports. Our main duty there was to get the drunks from the bars back to the ships. In Adak, Alaska, there was a fight on the bus: casualties included one ear and one finger; a good time was had by all.

In 1965, Earlene and I started our journey together. She was 17, I was 19. USCG pay was $270 a month, and we bought a motorcycle. (Well, I asked if she liked riding....) I was honorably discharged in March of 1967 and took a test with the city of LA for Assistant Steam Plant Operator, since I had experience with boiler operation. I passed the exam and was sent to a 2-week evaluation class. On the first day we were given an engineering type exam—math, power lines, electrical theory, and chemistry. I got a 29. The next morning, the instructor said that was the lowest anyone had ever scored, but each day the class would be tested on the operation, system design, steam cycle, generation, and switch-yard operations. He said if I scored well on these tests he would see about hiring me. The other folks didn't know much about power plants and "them things that make 'em work." At the end of the second week evaluation, I was #1 in the class. Well, that was not good, since now I would be working with these "other folks" for the next 30 years.

I thought I should get a high school diploma. I had the GED from the service, but a "real" one seemed better. I went to the local high school and explained my intent. I was told I needed to take all four years, so why not go to a 2-year college? They have to let you in, with the condition of scholastic probation. So, I signed up and finished with an AS in Engineering Tech.

Ok, so I left watching smoke stacks and water columns to be a Field Engineer Aide, a fancy title for a grunt on the survey party. I had no clue what the exam was like, but since I didn't want to score 29 again, I had taken the core Engineer classes, so now I could pass exams, get the GI Bill money, and we would be OK. For the younger readers, this was the heyday of "America In Transition" after the total rejection by a large majority of young people against the Vietnam War and the American political system. Now they had drugs and rich parents, and were looking for change.

Doug Jr. was born in 1970. I was finishing the 2-year course to transfer to a Power Engineering program at a 4-year school. We didn't know if we had enough money or could make it on the GI Bill funds, so I decided to finish the general ed classes at the 4-year state college and then transfer. This made sense until Dr. Thomas told a lady one night in a Philosophy class that yes, last week he explained X, the week before Y, and next week would be Z. She naively asked, "How do I know what the answer is?" He replied condescendingly, "Just ask me." What she didn't understand, but some of us did, was that we had to search for knowledge. There is no One Answer—just more searching.

So, after 5 years of that, I was searched out and the GI Bill money was done. I had finished the last semester taking a leave from work, needing two senior classes in three majors to get a BA. I promised I would never tell anyone I had a degree in Philosophy, Psychology, and that I studied functionalist theory in Sociology, or the current conflict theories going around, but if asked would mention a few observations of mine. My version: in 1975 I got a BA in How to cook Pancakes and understand Wages, Labor, Capital and What Plato Saw in the Cave.

In 1970, with a young family and a full load at school, I started surveying for a major power company. We walked, climbed, and dug holes to plant monuments or find monuments. We drove to remote locations and walked for hours looking for public land corners or power lines from Boulder/Hoover Dam to Los Angeles. I spent about 5 years in the San Joaquin Valley working on an environmental impact report for site development of a nuclear plant. We did subsidence measuring (a study of the stability of the area for ground movement). This required about 3,000 linear miles of second-order leveling. The project was voted out and we went south—or was it east?

The next major project was a 14-square mile power plant in Utah: laying out railroad track location for equipment and machinery delivery; building a short aqueduct; doing about 50 miles of second-order leveling; and then stringing a couple of power lines. Back to Los Angeles, we worked on roads, topography maps, right-of-way mapping, and property surveys. So, I spent a lot of time walking, climbing, digging, driving, and moving from town to town. We have lived in all of the towns on Interstate 15 from Victorville to just short of Salt Lake, plus many towns in Nevada and Central/Eastern California.

Our family traveled for 27 years. I joined a partnership and did private property surveys and parcel maps, subdivisions, and odd jobs as requested. Some we declined—like the call asking if we would "set up our equipment and act like we were surveying." (They had a property line dispute and wanted to scare the adjoining property owner.)

We also built custom houses, and later remodeled the Portal Store and built the Hostel. By the age of 17, Doug Jr. was Site Control Superintendent of our housing projects. He also worked with us on many of the private survey jobs. Earlene was the office manager, aka the lady everyone asked the hard questions: Is the job done? What is going on with the county/city, and When can you start the next project?

We juggled various projects concurrently, including site development for a large geothermal plant. More climbing, more leveling and mapping for just short of three years, and that's how we got to The Whitney Store. While traveling around we would live in our trailers, condos, apartments, camp out, live in the back of the trucks, or endless motels.

We were also resurveying all the power line right-of-ways and marking boundaries. This involved travel from LA to Las Vegas on the 15, and from LA to the Nevada border via Owens Valley along the 395. At one point we needed a place to stay as we moved from Bishop to Lone Pine, so we stopped at the local real estate offices and went in to see about rentals. I was reading the flyers on a bulletin board outside and saw the Store for sale. I made several calls and bought it. Earlene, Doug, my brother Larry, his wife Kathy, and their two sons Carl and Billy, came out to open the Portal Store for our first season in 1988.

We knew very little about the Portal, or how the Store was operated. We had several customers from the marketing profession ask if we would like some hints. One gentleman asked if I would get mad if he made some suggestions? I replied, "No." He told me he had been there three days and everything we did was wrong: you can't leave the store and go out climbing leaving a bag on the counter with money; you don't sell anything that people collect; you don't sell water or Gatorade; and you refuse to sell trendy clothing. And that was just the first day. He stayed several more days, and each day would offer additional observations. These types of customers gave us the basic business plan we wrote that first winter. We started a "wish list" at the counter and when someone would ask for something, we would write it down and search for the product.

I was asked to review a book on Mount Whitney some years ago at mid-season, a very busy time of the year. I had written down several pages of suggestions and called the person to recommend they revisit the area. Well, long story short, I will never review a book again.

So, what we draw our information from is a long road, and we've been down that road many times. We see repeated patterns, and yes, we also see a new "I've never seen that before" on a regular basis.

In a later chapter (See "When Something Goes Wrong," p. 57) we will introduce a list of recurring events that often lead to accidents, rescues, and recoveries—yes, body recoveries. These are also referenced throughout the book in parentheses, i.e. (potential for recovery) or (actual recovery).

— **Doug Thompson,** December 2018

Mt. Whitney from Thor Peak

1
CLIMBING THE MOUNTAIN

As a species, we are programmed to continually seek for something higher and better. Mt. Whitney symbolizes "The Top" of the world as we know it, and gives us an uncomplicated task that can be completed in a relatively short time with a fairly large payoff: "I did it! I climbed Mt. Whitney!"

People climb Mt. Whitney for many different reasons. Some have done it to win a bet. Many seek to accomplish a goal they have set or to prove themselves. Others do it regularly as a pilgrimage for spiritual renewal. It serves as an escape from the complexities of our mixed-up world and gets us back to the basics—left foot, right foot, breathe in, breathe out. Physical exertion relieves our mental and emotional stress, and there is a great view to reward us for persevering!

One of the attractions of Mt. Whitney is that it can be enjoyed at all levels. There are trails and hikes to fit every person's skills and abilities. A toddler or someone in a wheelchair can enjoy the area around Whitney Pond. A beautiful, lush trail follows the south side of Lone Pine Creek from the Pond down to the Whitney Portal Campground. This leisurely one-mile hike can quickly relax your nerves and provide a peaceful escape. The Whitney Trail is a strenuous route to the summit; but the first two and one-half miles up to Lone Pine Lake offer a good training ground for beginning hikers and include gorgeous views of Owens Valley. Another delightful variation is hiking the Trail by moonlight.

"I did it! Yeeeehaw!!"
- **VALENCIA, CA**

"Breathtaking from the top and the bottom"
- **RAMONA, CA**

Plan your trip around the full moon; you will find its light more than adequate, and will escape the heat of the day as well as the crowds. You will need a flashlight only in tree-shaded areas.

The Mountaineer's Route offers a good hike for "well-seasoned limbs," according to John Muir; and conquering the East Face, using ropes and special equipment, provides the rush that thrill-seeking climbers enjoy. For a description of the East Face climbs see Peter Croft's book, *The Good, The Great, and the Awesome*. Another challenge some have taken is a hike and/or bike ride from the lowest point in the continental U.S. (Badwater, in Death Valley, 282' below sea level) to the highest (Mt. Whitney)—both lie within Inyo County. You may choose to spend your whole summer in the mountains, following your dreams along the John Muir or Pacific Crest Trails, with Mt. Whitney being just a "tourist spot" along the way.

You are free to customize your visit to suit your needs and your schedule. We hope the information offered here will make it easier for you to plan and carry out your own Whitney Experience.

The essence of a wilderness experience includes going without some things, including a comfortable private bathroom with a flushing toilet. Since Mt. Whitney is THE most visited wilderness area in the Sierra, it naturally follows that lots of people have a need to relieve themselves along the Trail. When you pick up your permit, you'll be issued a "WAG Bag." Please honor the wilderness by carefully following all instructions, especially how to dispose of it properly after your hike.

The Whitney Trail is one of the best-kept routes in the Sierra. Originally built in 1904 through efforts of the local townsfolk in Lone Pine, it has been rebuilt and rerouted several times. Today it is the most heavily-traveled trail in the Sierra. This may give hikers the impression it is an easy trail, and for some it is. Do not forget, however, that it is rated "very strenuous," and people have lost their lives trying to hike it.

Due to the length and the altitude, it is an arduous one-day hike. Most people do better if they split it up, planning at least one overnight stay along the way. This section contains information about the Trail, including a guide pointing out landmarks along the way, common questions/answers, and special advice for those attempting to make the trip in one day.

Given the number of changes to visitor information, permit procedures, and web addresses since the last edition of this book, we recommend that you visit either our Whitney Portal forum website or the Whitney Portal Hostel & Hotel for current info.

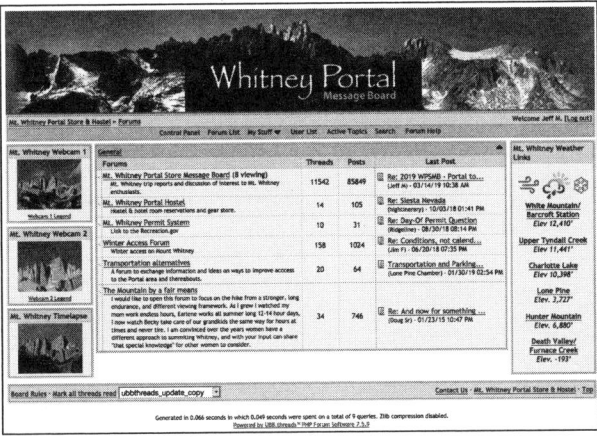

www.mountwhitneyforum.com

www.mountwhitneyportal.com

CLIMBING THE MOUNTAIN   3

A hiker on the slabs above Mirror Lake

CLIMBING FAQs

This section contains a compilation of our best answers to Questions Most Often Asked at the Whitney Store. We hope this list of Q&As helps. We have heard them more times than we can count. Most of the answers come from people like yourselves returning from a hike and telling us what they experienced.

1. **How far is it to the top?**
Most sources say it is 11 miles from the Portal to the summit. A more realistic way to look at this trail is to think of it as **22 miles round trip.**

2. **How long will it take ME to do it?**
Use as a guide: one hour per thousand feet elevation gain, plus two miles per hour distance. Six thousand feet elevation gain (6,000/1,000) = 6.0 hours, plus eleven miles distance (11/2) = 5.5 hours, suggesting a total of 11.5 or 12 hours for a one-way trip up. This trail is rated strenuous. On average, round trip is between 14-16 hours for some, others 16-20 hours. Not bad for a first time. Don't hurry/stress on the time since this may be your first time on a long hike at elevation. You want to go slow and take it easy the first 4-6 miles, saving the energy for the upper section, which is not any steeper (actually not as steep) but now at 12,000-14,000 ft. Above Consultation Lake, sun and altitude can be a problem. (See "How Long Will It Take" on p. 74)

"It's a long way"
- **LONDON, ENGLAND**

3. **Can we see Mt. Whitney from here?**
No. The mountain behind the Store is Thor Peak. The mountain to the south is Candlelight. If you travel back down the road to the first sharp

"One-day climb was great. The website helped a lot!"
- **SIMI VALLEY, CA**

turn (1/2 mile) you will see Mt. Whitney on the right and the Needles just to the left. If you look at a postcard from the Store, you'll see how it looks from this location.

4. Can we make it in a day?

Some can, some can't. You have to decide for yourself. Remember, distance isn't the problem for a good hiker. It is the altitude that seems to knock most people back. Also, the faster you travel, the less time your body has to adjust to the altitude. (See next chapter, "The Big One In One Day," p. 31)

5. How hot or cold is it on top?

General rule: four degrees for every 1,000 feet up. Six thousand feet elevation gain (6,000/1,000) = 6 x 4 = 24 degrees difference between the Portal and the top. So, if it's 60 degrees at the Portal, it's approximately 36 degrees on top.

Storms can come in very quickly. We have dropped 43 degrees in two hours at the Portal and have had snow in what was "shirt sleeve" weather. Wind can come up very fast and strong. On the back side (west) it can really add to fatigue and bring on hypothermia. Remember, at 40 degrees you are losing body heat faster than you can recover it if you're not protected from the elements.

Afternoon thunderstorms are rare most of the year but are not uncommon in July and August. You need to be ready for one at all times. Be prepared mentally to turn back if you face a storm. Lightning has been a problem on the mountain, especially when you are exposed on the ridges and above timberline. It has killed others and it can kill you.

6. Is the water safe to drink?

Maybe. Most water in the high country is safe. But some may not be, and some may vary based on the season. If you don't want to take a chance, boil, filter, or treat all your water before use. (If you are using a SteriPen, remember to take the cap off first!) Please don't "doo-doo" or pee in the water. It sounds stupid, but why do you think some water is bad now? One can always add 2-3 drops of 6% unscented bleach to a quart and let stand for 60 minutes (think of carrying 2 bottles, one being treated and one that was treated). Forget the bladder/tube/leak waiting to happen system. Hint $3.00 gallon of bleach will treat about 4,000 gallons. (See "Water Stops" on p. 120)

7. What should we take for an overnight trip?

If you are in a group, share—don't take five of everything. Take warm clothing, windbreakers, gloves, hats, and extra socks. Don't forget the sunscreen and sunglasses. Take at least one flashlight, good sleeping bags, ground pad, and ground cloth (plastic). Go as light as you can, but be prepared for a rapid change in the weather. Trim your toenails before you go. Wear shoes or boots that are well "broken in." Lighter boots, cowboy boots, or even sturdy tennis shoes are OK. The Trail is very rocky and may bruise unprotected feet. Bring moleskin. Watch for early signs of blisters and treat instantly. We see people with feet that would sell tickets at a carnival.

Pack weight is critical; my thoughts are, you should plan for a 2-night trip. One night makes no sense, because the energy to carry the weight to where you plan to camp for one night seems like it could be put into an easier one-day trip. The effect of moving that weight up the Trail may reduce the energy in your system; your hydration might not replenish overnight; and too few hours of restless sleep in the cold will weaken you, along with the effect of elevation. If you do plan an overnight trip, train with the pack weight you plan to carry. Do several uphill hikes with that pack—say Mt. Baldy in California from Manker Flat to the summit. This is about like the Portal to Trail Camp. But add 10 pounds, since you will lose the energy due to the elevation of Whitney.

8. When should I leave the Portal, and when should we reach Trail Camp?

The first two miles of the Whitney Trail can be very exposed to the elements, so it will be "Hot." After the logs, about two miles, you will be in the shadow of Candlelight peak, and to Mirror Lake there is tree coverage. The last stand of trees is just above Mirror Lake. Then you will be back in the sun, reaching about

11,000' and starting to slow down. Things will start to happen at this point. Straps will start to cut in. Blisters are forming, along with hot spots, rashes and friction burns, and you have 1-1/2 miles to reach Trail Camp while you bake in the sun until sundown. Then the cold will move in. Did I say, "Trail Camp is not the best choice?" I do not recall any AMS-HAPE-HACE studies that recommend going from sea level to 12,000' in one day.

9. How do we choose: Day hike vs. Overnight?

My own preference is a day hike at a nice slow pace, a "take the day" kind of trip. Leave at about 5:00 a.m., reach the summit by 3-4:00 p.m., and be back to the Portal by 10-11:00 p.m., making for a 16-18-hour day. See, I don't know about all the "afternoon thunderstorms" where you have to be off the summit before noon because someone told me. If it hasn't rained in the last five weeks, if there's no cloud in sight the night before, and the humidity in the Portal is the same, with no wind and no storms in the Gulf of Mexico moving around, I will risk an easy walk to the summit with one water bottle, a light day pack with some snacks, and a jacket.

Historically, overnight hikers trying to reach Trail Camp bonk around Trailside Meadow, 5 miles in and nearing 11,500'. Above the tree line, the Trail has transcended from crushed granite (DG) to mainly rock with steps. This makes the last mile to Trail Camp very slow. Many become frustrated, overheated and may start cramping.

If time allows, getting to the area several days before, spending time at 8,000', 10,000', and then 12,000' may help for the day hike. But by adding the weight of a backpack and sleeping at 12,000' feet without sufficient time to acclimatize, the overnight program tends to invite problems.

10. Do we need a permit?

Yes. Anyone in the Whitney Zone must now have a permit for both day and overnight hikes. For more information, visit this website: www.recreation.gov

11. Does anyone check for permits?

Yes. Rangers will turn you around if you do not have a permit, and they may impose a fine for each member of the group. Rangers are on the trails for your protection and enjoyment. Please follow all the rules and requirements in effect. The Trail is used very heavily and it takes very little to destroy the fragile alpine environment forever.

12. What is the best way to get to the top?

We can't stress this enough: It's a big mountain, a long distance. Weather, altitude, and your own mental and physical makeup are all factors you must consider. Arrive at the Portal a day or two before you start the hike, if possible. Rest. Get your pack ready. Try a very short shakedown walk. Get to bed early. Get up early. Do the first 2 miles before the sun gets too high—the first part of the Trail is open and can get quite warm. Walk at a pace so the slowest/weakest member of your party doesn't have to breathe hard. Also, don't hike so fast that you need to stop and rest, but do take a few minutes to rest about every hour.

Stop at Lone Pine Lake. Rest/sleep several hours. Continue to Outpost Camp—no hurry, pace yourself. Set up camp, organize your day pack for the ascent, and get to sleep early. Get up early and travel as light as possible. Take clothing/wind-breaker, sunglasses, sunscreen, water, snacks, and basic first aid supplies. Hike to the summit. Always try to stomach breathe (yoga breathing) on the way up, for the air is thin and we tend to not get enough air anyway. Enjoy the view and take a few moments to let what's around you happen. You have joined the silent family of people who have been on the mountain. Climbers often come up the various back routes, so please don't throw anything off the top. Hike back down to Outpost Camp. Most people continue on down to the Portal the same day.

"Oh, you mean this mountain..."
- **PALO ALTO, CA**

"Thanks for the great website & book—they helped me reach the summit!"
- **SAN JOSE, CA**

13. Do people steal packs/supplies left at Trail Camp or Outpost Camp?

Yes, but at times you can find people staying there who will watch your packs. The biggest thieves are the fat, furry marmots. Secure all food in your bear can, unless preparing or eating, to prevent raids by these cute but hungry snackers.

14. How is parking at the Portal?

Parking is always a problem on the weekends. The overflow lot was completed in 1990. This lot is about 500 ft. distance below the Portal area with direct access to the backpacker campground. Parking is impacted by long distance hikers leaving cars in the lots for weeks or months.

If you travel in a group on the Trail, and you or someone else decides to turn back, don't assume everyone will meet at the [any landmark in the area]. This causes a lot of problems. Many calls to Search and Rescue (SAR) could be avoided if people communicated about where they plan to meet. Please have a bailout plan so you can find each other. This will help prevent SAR volunteers from wasting their time and energy searching for you on the mountain when you are actually sleeping in your car.

15. Where can we camp, at or near the Portal?

You can camp for one night only at the backpacker campground, which has eighteen walk-in sites. Or, the Ravine campground, just below the backpacker's campground, has 10 sites (no reservation needed). Also, the Whitney Portal Family campground is about one mile down the road. They have 24 reservable sites, plus 18 non-reservable sites which are available on a first come first served basis. If they're full, try Lone Pine campground (43 sites), five miles down towards town. There are several other public, non-Forest Service campgrounds nearby:

1) Tuttle Creek (BLM), 85 sites
2) Portagee Joe (Inyo County), 15 sites
3) Diaz Lake (Inyo County), 200 sites.

16. When is the best time to hike to the top?

Some years, snow or ice stays on the switchbacks and Trail Crest until late June and nights are cool. July and August are crowded. The first week of September can be hot. The crowd clears out about the third week of September. From this time to the last of October is good, but be ready for an early snow or rapid weather change, and don't rely on people on the Trail for assistance. During the week is less crowded than on weekends. About the last of August, snowstorms start moving through and can cover the higher part of the Trail. If the Trail is covered with snow and ice, you are no longer just "hiking," and you should turn back if you are not prepared for the severest form of winter mountaineering.

Just come a few days early and your trip will be a great experience. You will have time to explore the area, and when you start the Trail it is something you are familiar with. This will allow time to set a nice pace with the group. Many want to get to the Portal a day before, jump out of the car and hike to Lone Pine Lake and back, and then hike Whitney the next day. This is not advised.

17. Do most people get sick?

Nearly everyone is affected by the altitude on this hike. Your symptoms may range from a mild headache to severe nausea, disorientation, or worse. Someone in your party should read about and understand altitude sickness. *Going Higher: The Story of Man and Altitude* by Charles S. Houston, M.D. published by Little, Brown and Company, is well worth having, not only for the information by the author, but also the 40 pages of bibliography.

18. What books or maps do we need?

This book probably covers everything you need to know. Check our website and message board at www.mountwhitneyforum.com, and talk with Rangers and/or hikers coming down for up-to-the-minute trail and weather conditions. Be sure to read the Forest Service handouts for current year information on trail conditions and bears. You can get to the top of Mount Whitney without a map, but we suggest an interactive app on your cellphone at least. A rough sketch of the route is included in the front of this book. If you want more detail, we carry excellent maps at the Store.

Map applications are a rapidly changing technology. Paper maps are now becoming collectors' items. I think a simple one-page topo map should be taken, but I know many hikers may not have experience with map reading and since the Trail is developed, my choice would be an interactive map app—one that shows the Trail, topo, and your location in real time. Most people have smart phones that will access mapping software that can be downloaded prior to the trip. I like In-Reach by Garmin—not a GPS unit, just the inexpensive app for your phone that has GPS data if you turn on your location. OK, so your phone will go dead. Try turning off between checking your location…OK, it is endless. Bring a power cell as a backup power supply. You can use your camera/phone and LED light the entire trip.

19. Do I really need to allow some time at the Portal before my hike?

Some critical reasons to arrive days early—NOT to acclimate —but to find:
1) The Trailhead
2) The bathrooms
3) The walk-in campgrounds
4) Where to park
5) Food storage
6) To talk with people coming off the Trail
7) To take a drive to Horseshoe Meadow and spend a few hours there at 10,000 ft

Sleep in town. Next morning drive east to Bristlecone Forest— you can drive to 12,000 ft. Take a short hike at the end of the road. Hike out to the turnouts looking westerly to the Sierra and the Valley below. Again, sleep low back in town. Get your permit (and WAG Bag), have a solid meal, and get a full night's sleep! Do you sleep in the dirt at home? Do you get up at 1:00 a.m., wandering around in the dark looking for green eyes/blue eyes/yellow eyes in the trees? Listen to the car doors slamming, car alarms going off, people yelling at the rest of the party, "Where are Mike and Mary?" Wondering if the hogs ate them when they went to the bathroom? "I couldn't find the light switch in the bathroom!"

Plan on spending several days in the area to reduce the anxiety level. Say you are the "leader." You direct the group to meet at the portal at 1:37 a.m. Of course, you don't know where the trailhead is. You by chance meet most of the group wandering around in the dark. Now the hunt for the trailhead starts. You have searched the Internet and have at least five different locations of where it may be. It's by the bathroom (so which of the three?). It is in front of the waterfall. No, it's behind the store. No, it's over by the bridge. Wait, "What is that thing?" The trailhead, of course! The sign that says, "Mount Whitney Trail." Now, the Trail is not well maintained—the first 100 ft., that is. Recall you are the leader, and after losing about 30 minutes looping around the Portal several times, that team member you thought wouldn't even show up has found the trailhead.

You need to make up for lost time ... Now the race starts!

20. Are there bears?

Yes. American Black Bears (they are not all black; they're also commonly found in brown, grey, or cinnamon). During the 1988 season, bears started showing up for supper at the Store. They can and will rip open your car while you're on the mountain. They recognize most food items by sight and smell. Most people underestimate their strength and ability to search and destroy. Bears are pretty routine at Outpost Camp, and were sighted at Trail Camp beginning in 2000. During the season, Forest Service Rangers check regularly to make sure all campers store their food in bear-proof containers. This is now a requirement, and you can be fined for not abiding by it. You must store food properly to keep it away from the animals. While your car is at the

"It is good having a store at this place!"
- **KERTOGENBOSCH, NETHERLANDS**

"Great little store & Mtn."
- **SMITHFIELD, UT**

Portal, keep all food in the metal bear boxes provided. If a bear breaks into your vehicle, you may be cited, and your car towed off the mountain. Bears are less of a problem now on average, but they are still active.

21. What services are available at the Store?

We serve breakfast, lunch, and dinner. We sell milk, cold drinks, ice, and beer. We try to keep last-minute hiking and fishing supplies on hand: water purifying equipment, socks, sunscreen, walking sticks, bear cannisters, bait, tackle, energy drinks, and snacks. We also offer souvenir items developed by the Store or for the Store: T-shirts, mugs, patches, hats, spoons, postcards, cedar boxes, and much more. We maintain a bulletin board and will try to pass information up the Trail by word of mouth. Also, we try to keep a daily report of the Trail and weather by people like you stopping in and giving us updates. Our location has limited cell service. If you can't connect, don't give up on the first try—walk around the area or go down the road a little way, and you may find a signal. Yes we sell trinkets and cook hamburgers, but we are not in charge of anything outside the Store or our permitted operating area. **Please note: We do not have permits.** You need to stop at the Eastern Sierra Interagency Visitor Center just south of Lone Pine (at the corner of Highway 395 and Highway 136) to pick up your permit before you head up to the trailhead.

22. Do I have to drive all the way to Whitney Portal to get one of your T-shirts?

Nope. You can order items all year round through our website at: **www.mountwhitneyportal.com**

Also, we have a second store and Hostel/Hotel right on Route 395 in Lone Pine. It's located at:

238 South Main Street,
Lone Pine, CA.
Telephone: 760-876-0030.

The Mount Whitney Portal Hostel and Hotel is a great place to stay. Choose between bunk beds (dormitory rooms) or private hotel rooms, according to your budget. It has a view of Mt. Whitney, but being in town, it allows for walking to restaurants and stores. There's a lobby area to gather your party, and a store if you've forgotten something or need a souvenir. There are showers for hikers too, if that's all you need. The Hostel also offers an area to do trainings and/or workshops.

The Whitney Portal Hostel & Hotel in Lone Pine

A dayhiker coming down the Switchbacks

THE BIG ONE IN ONE DAY

People constantly ask us for advice when planning or attempting to hike to the summit of Mt. Whitney and back in one day. Information in this chapter will help you accomplish the one-day climb. However, most of these suggestions apply to overnight hikers as well.

There are benefits and drawbacks to doing the whole hike in one day. The greatest benefit is that you don't have to haul overnight gear up the trail. It gives you a great sense of satisfaction to "do it" in one day. It also saves time if you are on a tight schedule. On the other hand, it is a demanding hike—people should know what they are getting into before attempting it. And, as with any hurried encounter with the wilderness, you will miss out on some of the subtle beauties and the deeper connection that sleeping on the mountain can bring.

What You Are Facing

People who want to successfully climb Mount Whitney in a day have three formidable adversaries to overcome:

1) High Elevation
2) Dehydration
3) Exhaustion

Each can be a challenge, but there is much you can do to overcome them. Also:

4) Hypothermia can confront you at night, during storms, or at colder times of the year.

1) High Elevation
- On the summit of Mount Whitney, the amount of oxygen getting into your system is 20% less than at sea level.

"Drink lots of H_2O"
- CHULA VISTA, CA

"Nice hike, major headache at top"
- FAIRFIELD, CA

- High Altitude Illness (HAI) happens when your body doesn't get enough oxygen into the bloodstream. Symptoms are headache, weakness, fatigue, loss of reasoning ability, upset stomach, vomiting, and incoherence.
- HAI can appear as low as 6,000' and includes three conditions (see *Going Higher*, by Dr. Houston for detailed information):

    1) Acute Mountain Sickness (AMS)

    2) High Altitude Pulmonary Edema (HAPE—fluid accumulation in lungs)

    3) High Altitude Cerebral Edema (HACE- fluid accumulation in brain)
- Risk factors for HAI include:
    - Dehydration
    - Prior history of HAI
    - Living below 3,000' altitude
    - Exertion
    - Preexisting cardiopulmonary conditions (for example, PFO—Patent Foramen Ovale, or PDA - Patent Ductus Arteriosus - heart valves not closing properly after birth. Present in 20-30% of adults and often not diagnosed due to lack of symptoms)
- Physical fitness is not protective against HAI.
- Preventive measures against HAI:
    - Acclimatize before climbing—this is the most effective
    - Ginkgo biloba before climbing may reduce symptoms
    - Aspirin taken every 4 hours may prevent headaches
    - Ask your doctor about these prescription meds:

        Diamox (acetazolamide) 125-250 mg taken 3 times a day shortly before and during ascent can reduce symptoms. Do not take this medication if you are allergic to sulfa drugs. It is a mild diuretic and may work by changing the body's acid-base balance and stimulating breathing.

Decadron (dexamethasone) 8 mg once a day has also been shown to be effective. However, this steroid medication may have more adverse effects.

Various inhalers (bronchodilators/rescue inhalers, and/or long-term/control inhalers)

Bottled oxygen results are inconclusive

- During the climb:
  - Ibuprofen is usually very effective
  - Ginkgo biloba, aspirin, Diamox or Decadron may help relieve symptoms

Our personal preference is to adapt naturally, versus "tricking" the body with chemicals. We don't recommend using anything that would mask your body's natural warning system. If possible, sleep at a higher elevation before your hike. The best method is to spend the day high (above 10,000 ft.), and sleep low, but if you live and work along the coast you can drive into the 5,000–8,000 ft. mountains and spend the night.

We have seen hikers standing on the Trail with eyes glazed, unable to speak clearly. These people should be taken down to lower altitudes without delay, but most will argue that they are OK and that they HAVE to make it to the top. The longer they stay, and the higher they go, the sicker they will get. This condition can be FATAL—get down to lower altitude IMMEDIATELY if you or anyone in your group develops these symptoms.

2) Dehydration

- Hydrate as much as possible several days before your hike. Not just with water, but electrolytes too.
- Being at high altitude causes you to lose far more fluids than at lower elevations.
- Dehydration compounded by low vapor pressure of oxygen results in changes in blood chemistry, making it more acidic and harder to absorb what oxygen is available.
- You won't feel like drinking; if you get dehydrated, you'll feel even less like drinking. Drink anyway.

DEHYDRATION AND STRESS
(source: American Red Cross)

Fluid Loss (% Body Weight)	Normal Temperatures	High Temps and/or Strenuous Exercise
1-2%	Impaired Judgement, Irritability, Headache, Muscular Aches	Sweating, Erythema (flushed face)
3%	Thirst reflex initiated, Lassitude, Sense of Fatigue, Loss of Appetite, Tight Sore Muscles	Profuse Sweating, Noticeably (to others) Impaired Judgement & Confusion*
4-6%	Profound Thirst, Dizziness, Muscle Cramps, Weakness, Fatigue	Very Irritable, may be Irrational, Pale, Severe Headache, especially at base of skull*
7-8%	Nausea, Vomiting, Severe Vertigo or Dizziness, somewhat Irrational, Severe Muscle Cramps, Staggering	Cold, Clammy Skin even though core temperature may be 104 degrees F or higher, May have Stopped Sweating*
9-10%	Collapse, Very Irrational, Unconscious	Pale skin, Tense & Contracted Muscles, Pupils may be Dilated, Weak & Rapid Pulse, Low Blood Pressure, Shallow Respiration*

*Stages of **Heat Exhaustion**

DEHYDRATION AND STRESS
(source: American Red Cross)

Fluid Loss (% Body Weight)	Normal Temperatures	High Temps and/or Strenuous Exercise
8-10+%	**Heat Stroke:**	Skin Red, Dry & Hot Sweating has Stopped, Severe Headache, Extremely Weak, Numbness & Tingling in Extremities, Muscles Tense & Convulsive, Confusion, Dark Urine (if any), Pupils Contracted, Pulse Strong & "pounding," Rapid, Shallow & Labored Respiration Delirious Unconscious Comatose

- Snow is water; use a wide mouth container so you can add it if needed. However, add only in amounts that will melt; too much and you'll freeze the water in your bottle.
- Sucking on snow will give you some moisture but note that it also lowers your core body temperature.
- We recommend taking a liter and filtering water along the way to replace it. Strive for intake of at least a half-liter or more every hour, or at least one liter every 1,000 feet.
- Dehydration results in classic symptoms of heat exhaustion: muddled thinking, irritability, fatigue.

We like to add a package of electrolyte replacement drink to two quarts of water. This has been found to reduce leg cramps and loss of overall energy. (Doug also places a small pebble in his mouth to keep the moisture machine working.) During the heat of the day, cut a lemon and suck the juice. This will clean your mouth so when you do drink you will taste the water and quench your thirst. At stream crossings, wet the back of your neck and hair to help cool down. Water is available up to 12,000 feet. From Trail Camp to the summit and back can be free of snow and runoff. Make sure you leave Trail Camp with enough water: two quarts bare minimum.

A runner who spent his two-week summer vacations backpacking in the Sierra shared this story: Each year, after the first day, he would have a splitting headache and malaise, no appetite, feel lousy and often nauseous. He figured that it went with the high-altitude experience. One year, he took some electrolyte replacement with him. He drank at least a quart every day, had none of the symptoms, and covered much more territory than ever before.

Mountaineering expeditions report that these supplements/drinks help them keep going even above 20,000' with no muscle cramps or altitude sickness, and less fatigue even with 100-lb packs.

3) Exhaustion

- Climbing Mount Whitney in a day is strenuous—harder than running a marathon, according to some who have done both.
- Eat lots of carbohydrates and get lots of rest (no partying) in the days before your hike.
- Your body is a machine; don't run it on empty. Put fuel in the tank.
- Pace yourself. Don't go so fast that you must stop and rest often. Do stop and rest for 5-10 minutes every hour. Drink and eat each time.
- Hiking poles are invaluable. Use two.
- Try for one mile per hour going up (10-11 hours) and about 2 mph going down (5 hours) = 16-hour day.
- Go as light as possible.

- Strive for nibbling all day while hiking, vs. stopping for larger meals.
- Calories are most important. Don't worry about ratios of proteins/carbs/fats.
- When possible, eat carbs; these are utilized most quickly. However, any food that tastes good to you is better than things that are "healthy" but stay in your pack due to appetite loss.
- Bring and eat what YOU like = things you are more apt to tolerate at altitude. Examples: jerky, candy bars (chocolate can get messy), lemon drops, jellybeans, cheese, nuts. Take a treat or two for yourself.
- Use electrolyte additives with hydration. But make sure the product you decide to use is tested on many previous hikes, and note that some of the ingredients may be used in laxatives.
- An instant cup of soup or tea can warm your body and your spirits (you'll need a small stove).

You are at the starting line of a marathon when you attempt Mt. Whitney in one day. However, unlike a marathon with gentle ups and downs, the Trail is continuously up and continuously down, 10.7 miles up and 10.7 miles back. This puts an extended load on your muscles and other body parts, using them for a much longer period of time than you normally train. In order to condition your body accordingly, you would need to do the stair walker for about seven hours, then turn around and use a completely different system of muscles walking down an uneven trail with steps up to 18 inches high and a steep downward slope. Don't assume that because you worked out faithfully for 45 minutes daily that you will be in condition to hike to the summit in one day.

Never leave LA and drive to Whitney, sleep a couple of hours, jump up and take off up the trail. This is the most common formula for failure. Try

> "Be comfortable with and have faith in all your gear before your big day."
> - **MESSAGE BOARD**

> "Make sure to wear sunscreen."
> - **LOS ANGELES, CA**

to spend at least a full day at Whitney Portal. Get a good night's rest and start your hike about one hour earlier than you would normally get up. Waking up three hours before your body is expecting it will be hard.

If you leave the Portal around 5:00 a.m. you should be back by 10:00 p.m. The last 2.5 miles (Lone Pine Lake to the Portal) are well lighted by reflections off the bright granite. You must be in this area by dark. From Trail Camp to Lone Pine Lake is very rocky, uneven, and not well marked—you don't want to hike it in the dark. You should leave the summit by 4-5 p.m. (July-Aug) to make Lone Pine Lake by about dark.

4) Hypothermia

Hypothermia is a condition where the body loses more heat than it can generate to keep your internal organs warm. Lowering your core temperature causes loss of reasoning ability. It also causes severe shivering and loss of motion—you just want to stay put—and you may lapse into sleep. If your body temperature continues to drop, death can and will occur. This is why it is critical to travel with someone.

All members of your party must know the effects/symptoms of hypothermia. Stay dry and never let anyone with hypothermic symptoms lie down and go to sleep. Once your body starts shaking, get warm! Add clothing, head gear, and upper body (chest area) direct body contact. Do not ignore these symptoms! Drink hot liquids, do jumping jacks, and get down to a camp where you can stay warm!!! Never stop treating for heat loss until they have recovered and are down to a safe area.

What You Should Bring

Everything listed can be discussed for hours—how/why take this, and not that. Here are some parameters:
- Know that no one took you up the mountain and no one should be required to take you down.
- Take enough to get yourself back down to the trailhead in the dark and in a snowstorm.

- Keep weight to an absolute minimum.
- Know your limits of physical and mental endurance.
- Get a day use permit (a WAG Bag will be issued when you pick up your permit).

Going Light
- Select gear and clothing with weight in mind.
- Go for a tune-up hike (at least 15 miles) and pretend it's Whitney. When you get home, divide your pack into three piles: stuff you used all the time, stuff you used a little, stuff you didn't use. Get rid of piles #2 and #3, while staying safe (i.e., don't throw out your first aid kit just because you didn't use it)
- If you can take 10 pounds out of your pack before you start, that is 10 pounds you don't have to carry up 6,200'. Ten pounds can mean the difference between making the top with a smile, and puking your guts out halfway up the switchbacks.

A one-day trip up Whitney isn't the time or place to test out a new piece of clothing or equipment. Everything you take and everything you do to prepare for this hike is critical. Most of the high dollar products, poly-whatever, etc., are hyped up by slick ad magazines. Do not bring any of these if you have not used and tested them yourself. Before you spend those hard-earned dollars, make the salesperson look you in the eye and tell you they would pay full price and risk their lives on it. You cannot buy security, you have to earn it yourself.

Consider the items you already have in your closet before you rush off to go shopping. We see people who spend hundreds of dollars for special clothing, thinking it will help them. If the weather gets bad on your one-day hike, you need to turn around and come down the mountain whether you're wearing new stuff or not.

"Whitney in one day, brutal but beautiful!"
- SANTA ROSA, CA

Here is what Doug wears: long pants, lightweight hiking boots, T-shirt, long-sleeved button shirt (light color), and sunglasses. He brings a day pack—a fanny pack or book bag—containing the following:

- Wool sweater, hat (balaclava), and gloves
- Extra-large trash bag (poncho or emergency sleeping bag)
- Windbreaker
- Sunscreen (use especially on nose and top of ears). Above 11,000 feet you are exposed to sun without protection of trees. The sun burns right into you from reflection off snow and rock. The atmosphere is thin and second-degree sunburn can happen fast.
- Hat with a brim (helps prevent sunburn on scalp and face)
- Flashlight w/extra batteries/bulb
- A very small propane stove with one pot/cup
- During June, Sept. or colder months, he adds a down vest or jacket, and long underwear

Ground Rules

Never go alone! Go up together and come down all the way together. If your party separates (due to injury, fatigue, etc.), keep at least two in each subgroup. Set a pace that you can keep all day without stopping. Deep breathe. This takes practice but is a real help above 11,000 feet.

All of this is based on using your own common sense and your awareness of your own limitations. You should see a doctor and make sure you are in good health before starting this climb. Talk with your doctor about Diamox (a prescription that can alleviate altitude sickness) and any conditions you might have that could be affected by high altitude.

Many people have tried to set and break records (their own or others') for this one-day trip. Others just show up and take off, many coming into the Store afterward to reflect on their experience—how far they got, when they got sick, when the first blister showed up, when they realized how much slower you go at higher elevations, and how cold it got so fast. Remember: the important thing is not how long it took to get to the summit and back. It is the experience you had that day you took the walk that will stay with you all your life.

After 30 years of experience on the mountain, here are some suggestions that may be useful:

One Day Tips: For mid-June to mid-September
- Arrive several days before your planned hike
- Pick up your hiking permit and WAG Bag

Day 1:
- Visit Horseshoe Meadow, 10,000 ft.
- Sleep in town/valley

Day 2:
- Visit Bristlecone Pines, 12,000 ft.
- In the afternoon, take a trip to the Whitney Portal to find the trailhead
- Sleep in town/valley
- Reduce pack weight to minimum
- Make sure you have poles, sunscreen, light gloves and head gear

Day of Hike
- Start at 4 – 6:00 a.m. for Day Hike
- Avoid using fancy bladder systems as their additional pack and gadgets are dead weight.
- Take very short breaks—snack as you hike.

> *"I didn't even have the energy to chew my energy bars. I eventually got them down and within an hour I sprang back to life"*
> - **MESSAGE BOARD**

Trail Crest can be a great summit point

- Check the sky for weather changes and ask hikers as they are coming down about conditions.
- Set the pace about 1 mile per hour and stay in a group.
- Resupply water and electrolyte at each location (See Water Stops, page 120).
- Trailside Meadow: Drink water and electrolytes.
- Now start using pressure breathing and lock-knee rest step.
- Time check at Trail Camp 5-6 hours—any problems?
- Switchbacks number 22-25: get water if flowing.
- Look east, not up.
- Trail Crest: look west for weather changes. Time check: 7-8 Hours.
- Please note: Trail Crest is a great summit point! Don't bother going to the top if you are struggling and/or behind schedule; going to the summit will add 5-6 hours to a long day and can turn a pleasant hike into a "death march."
- JMT Junction: could drop packs, carry just water and a windbreaker if weather is calm.

- Maintain slow steady pace to summit.
- Check group for problems, head down watching for loose rocks and slick slabs; use poles extended to break shock.
- Continue on down getting water as needed, eating snacks and taking breaks.
- If exhausted, lie down in the dirt and sleep; take a power nap.
- Don't become a walking disaster, and risk walking off the trail!

One More Big-One-In-One-Day Success Story

"This was my first attempt at climbing Mount Whitney. I'm 26 years old and have wanted to take this hike for 10 years. With the right knowledge, encouragement, and support, I made it in under 24 hours, going with seven friends.

I would like to encourage anyone with the desire, to make this hike a reality for themselves. If I can do it, I believe anyone can!"
— Rochelle K.

"Rochelle worked late the night before her hike. She got off at 11:00 p.m. and came up to the Portal. Our group took off shortly after midnight. We made several rest stops along the way, arriving at the summit around 11:00 a.m. As usual, going down was more taxing since everyone had been awake for so many hours. We all arrived at the Store before closing time."
— Douglas B.

Rochelle's successful experience is one more example of how the information in this book can increase your chances of attaining your goal to climb Mount Whitney. Whether you choose the one-day hike or an overnight trip, take the time to study and apply the advice herein.

Please be safe, and enjoy!

Looking southeast
from the summit

TRAIL GUIDE

Climbing Mt. Whitney is like eating a Whitney Portal Store pancake—at first, the task seems overwhelming. However, you can break it up into manageable pieces. Take the Trail one segment at a time, and always remember that the distance you are hiking up the Trail must be doubled to allow for your return trip. Use this trail guide for a day hike or an overnight trip.

We've added some descriptive visualization as a tool to help you relax and prepare mentally as you study this guide.

Trailhead: Mile 0.0, 8,367 feet el.

The Whitney Trail begins about 100 feet east of the Store—look for steps leading up to the bulletin boards where the Forest Service posts information (you can too—messages for other hikers, lost & found, etc.) At first, the Trail leads away from the mountain. Don't let this confuse you—it soon makes a sharp turn back to the west and leads you through a series of switchbacks taking you up through a pleasant grove of pine trees. Chances are you will soon be peeling off outer layers of clothing due to the exertion of climbing and the warmth of the morning sun.

Visualization: Let's assume you spent several days at higher elevation (above 8,000') and are on your way up the Trail (permit in hand). Let's start the visualization process—seeing the granite walls, the waterfall, the trees and the valley below, with the Inyo Mountains to the east. Feel the cool morning air surrounding you and hear the busy activity of the squirrels and birds as you walk, feeling relaxed and full of energy, knowing the day will be pleasant and enjoyable.

"It's a beautiful trail & lots of comaraderie!"
- **REDLANDS, CA**

CLIMBING THE MOUNTAIN   31

Carillon Drainage: Mile 0.5

Depending on the weather and the time of year, a little mud or a few inches of water cross the Trail here. The growth thickens, giving more shade.

Visualization: Take a deep breath and enjoy the feeling of stepping into the wilderness and away from whatever you do for a living.

First Serious Stream Crossing: Mile 0.65

The North Fork of Lone Pine Creek gurgles across the Trail here. Stepping stones offer a dry crossing later in the season. You can walk through the water too. Be careful! Beginning backpackers without boulder-hopping experience should be especially cautious. We have seen a lot of people who lose their footing here, resulting in a sprain or broken bone. Ice can make the rocks extra slippery on cold mornings. While it usually melts during the day, it may ice up again by late afternoon, causing a hazard for tired hikers hurrying down the last stretch.

Visualization: The first stream crossing gives you a chance to either rock-hop or just walk through the flow. Hear the rush of the water and feel the mist in the air, creating a calm and peaceful respite.

Entrance to John Muir Wilderness: Mile 0.85, 8,480 feet el.

The sign tells you where you are and what regulations you are expected to follow. Before your trip, visit www.recreation.gov or mountwhitneyforum.com for current information on permit requirements.

Visualization: Read the sign and start your journey up a series of switchbacks that will take you from the north side of the canyon to the south side. Look at the waterfall on the south side and follow this silver ribbon into the trees. The Trail goes across an open area where one can see the effects of winter and wind. Look for tree tops that have snapped in the wind, and observe how snow *pushing on the trees has forced them to grow with a permanent bend.*

The Trail offers many beautiful views of Owens Valley to the east, as well as spectacular granite walls and peaks to the north and south. By now you will realize that whether or not you go to the summit, your trip has been worthwhile. You will see hikers with all varieties and extremes of gear. Some folks cover this part of the Trail in shorts, T-shirts, and sandals, carrying nothing but a bottle of water. Others sport heavy boots, snow suits, and 60-pound packs with every conceivable piece of climbing equipment dangling off their backs. It all depends on how long you'll be in the wilderness, and what you're planning to do there. At one point, Lone Pine Creek provides a lovely gushing waterfall. Most people cannot resist the urge to snap a photo or two, but save some shots for later.

Visualization: Look up and to the right—there you will see the rock work on the trail, and above it the slanting face of Thor Peak. Turning to your left, Owens Valley opens into full view. Look for the green ribbon on the far side of the valley that is the Owens River bed. Notice the color on the Inyo Mountains. As you cross to the south side of the canyon, you will pass through a ¼ mile display of flowers and ferns. Try to identify as many as you can. This area is over 9,000' in elevation and some of the plants will take a different size and shape.

As you approach Lone Pine Lake, the Trail levels off. On your return hike down, this is where people coming up will inevitably ask, "How much farther is it to Lone Pine Lake?"

Visualization: You will come upon a series of logs that cross a small stream, just past a beautiful waterfall and a very large display of corn lilies.

"Lone Pine Lake on his own feet!
- age 3"
- LANCASTER, CA

Look around the logs as you cross, and you should see trout swimming about. Continue up the Trail through a nice stand of fir, where it takes you to the sandy area above Lone Pine Lake. This flat area allows you to stretch your legs out and prepare for the next section.

Lone Pine Lake: Mile 2.8, 9,420 feet el.

A sign on a post points to Lone Pine Lake, which lies at the end of a short trail forking left and down. You should take the time to enjoy this scenic spot—reward yourself for getting this far. Camping is allowed here (200 ft. away from the water, and with an overnight permit), and if you're not in a hurry it's a good place to acclimate for a night. Mosquitoes are a problem at times. The lake offers beautiful reflections of the slope to the south, the trees, and the sky. Soak your feet in the cool water, or take the plunge and go for a refreshing swim. Refill your water bottle, and continue hydrating to replenish fluids. This is also a great spot for fishing.

Visualization: *At the back of this draw the Trail switchbacks to the right and into Outpost Camp. As you walk this section, look to the east; enjoy the reflecting pool of Lone Pine Lake, and the valley beyond.*

Big Horn Sheep Park: Mile 3.5

After a short climb past Lone Pine Lake, the Trail soon levels out to a sandy area and the entrance to the Whitney Zone at 2.75 miles. Further travel requires a permit for both dayhikes and overnight trips. From this point the Trail then follows a ledge system up to the entrance of a large meadow: Big Horn Sheep Park. New maps show it as Bighorn Park; it has also been called Big Horn Flat or Ibex Flat. The Trail crests at the east end of the meadow (a good photo spot for a view back down to Lone Pine Lake). A welcome downhill stretch leads into the Park. At one time this area was a base for pack trains. The Trail has been rerouted along the south side of the Flat due to "free-for-all" tramps across the meadow that nearly destroyed it in the 70's.

Visualization: *As you enter Outpost Camp area, the Trail drops into a meadow alive with flowers and activity. The Trail follows the southerly side of the meadow. At the west end you will see a magnificent waterfall where the Trail bears right into Outpost Camp.*

Outpost Camp: Mile 3.8, 10,360 el.

Congratulations—you have passed the 10,000' elevation level! Outpost Camp is located at the west end of Big Horn Sheep Park. This area is ideal for camping due to its level spaciousness and lovely shade trees. Lone Pine Creek provides a large and beautiful waterfall (and plenty of drinking water) just to the south. A day hike to the summit can be made from this spot, leaving behind the extra pounds of overnight gear. This camping area is always less crowded than Trail Camp, more esthetically pleasing, and offers much better protection from wind and cold.

Visualization: *There is another water crossing here that again can be "hopped" via stones, or you can walk through it. A short distance ahead you will see the next section of short switchbacks.*

Mirror Lake: 4.3 mi., 10,640 el.

The Trail climbs steeply up a series of switchbacks to Mirror Lake. While overnight camping is prohibited here, it is a pleasant rest stop. Fishing is a possibility as well as swimming (although the water is always cold). Another series of switchbacks climbs up to the south, providing photogenic views of Mirror Lake from above. At this point the Trail becomes very rocky, and trees thin out as you approach timber line.

As the Trail curves west, more views of Owens Valley below invite you to use your camera. Make sure you drink water as you continue to climb. It will help minimize effects of the altitude, and drainage along this part of

"It's not how far you go but what you learn along the way"
- ST. THOMAS, USVI

the Trail offers many opportunities to refill your jugs. Say goodbye to trees as you pass the last few twisted specimens.

Visualization: Soon you will arrive at the east end of Mirror Lake. During peak runoff periods, the rock stairs are covered with water and you will need to walk along the edge of the rock, heading for the sign: "Mirror Lake—No Camping." Now travel up and left to the next set of switchbacks. This leads you through the last stand of trees and on to the granite slabs that bring you to Trailside Meadow.

Trailside Meadow: 5.3 mi., 11,395 el.
Formerly known as Ram Horn Park, this colorful little area provides a welcome visual relief from bare rocks, granite, snow, and sky. Lone Pine Creek flows through it, watering the many wildflowers and shrubs. Marmots live here, and may entertain you with their whistles and "woofs." Rangers are often seen here too—make sure you can find your Wilderness Permit if they ask to see it. No overnight camping is allowed.

Visualization: Drink in the beauty above and below as you pass through this lovely spot. Listen to the cooling, rushing stream from Consultation Lake, and spend a few minutes looking at the fledgling flowers against the stark rock. Notice how great you feel, and be aware of how easy it has been drawing in energy and exhaling tension with every breath.

Consultation Lake: 5.8 mi.
This is the most misunderstood lake on the Whitney Trail. Some people call it "Constellation" Lake. Although this name is prettier, it is incorrect, as is "Consolation Lake." Consultation Lake is located to the left and above the Trail, about a half mile before Trail Camp. Exhausted hikers who are concentrating on putting one foot in front of another, and on continuing to breathe, may miss it altogether. The unnamed ponds at Trail Camp are often mistaken for Consultation Lake.

For those who have the energy and inclination to explore,

there are several campsites at and above this beautiful lake which are cleaner and less hectic than Trail Camp.

Visualization: The Trail now moves on to another set of switchbacks that exits at Trail Camp. As you walk through this area, the ridge line surrounds you and the giants start to appear before your eyes. You are now at 12,000' and the towering granite face is only a stone's throw away.

Trail Camp: 6.3 mi., 12,039 feet el.

This is the most popular camping spot on the Trail. While there are some good arguments for spending the night here, there are also many reasons for finding another place to sleep. Trail Camp is ideally located for two-day hikers because it puts them in the right place for a fresh start in the morning. The trouble is, so many people stay there that it has become polluted. During the busiest season, this camp is crowded, noisy, and it stinks!

Another reason to avoid using Trail Camp as your base is the harsh weather conditions. Violent winds have destroyed tents or blown them away. The lack of topsoil means there is no dirt to anchor tent stakes. There may be snow on the ground until mid-July. By late August, storms can blow in suddenly, leaving a blanket of up to six inches of snow. It is a rocky, barren place—a little like camping on the moon (except for the water). The pond may have WAG Bags floating around.

Unfortunately, some marmots have made a living off the leftovers at Trail Camp. Bear canisters are REQUIRED. Don't share snacks with these cute little guys, either purposely or by accident—it's not the best thing for their health.

"Climb on, Dude!"
- FLAGSTAFF, AZ

"Very hard but glad that I made it"
- DALLAS, TX

At busy times, this Camp is also polluted with the sounds of portable speakers, and loud voices. Be respectful of others and of the wilderness. Bright lights are also an unwelcome distraction. A small flashlight is essential (unless the moon is full), but bright lanterns are out of place.

Water sources at Trail Camp are the most likely to require purification treatment. You'll need to tank up for your climb to the summit. There is a possible water source about one-third up the switchbacks, depending on the time of year and the time of day.

Visualization: *As you walk towards the west, you can see the Trail going up the slope first to the south, then to the north, to catch Trail Crest.*

Switchbacks: 6.5-8.5 mi., 12,039-13,777 feet el.

Some people will tell you the switchbacks are easy, and others say it's the hardest part of the climb. One thing most everyone agrees on—they're boring! How many switchbacks are there? While that all depends on what exactly you count as a "switchback," the number is somewhere between 98 and 100. This part of the Trail is smooth and well-constructed, making it often possible to swing your legs, giving momentum for each successive step. Typically, there is snowmelt running across the Trail at regular intervals, and you should continue to drink water. Polemonium, a high-altitude, deep purple wildflower, spruces up the decor if you are climbing in July or August.

There are cable railings along a steep area of the Trail. While they were installed to provide help and safety along the way, use caution. Now the cables are in bad repair and if the Trail is covered with snow/ice, they will not be of much value. Ice can be a problem on the switchbacks, and these railings sometimes give hikers a false sense of security. This is another spot where accidents happen due to early morning or late afternoon ice on the trail, or on the railings themselves.

Some years, snow covers the switchbacks as late as mid-July. It is impossible to follow this route until it has melted. The alternative is a chute just to the north of the switchbacks, which can be climbed in snow by experienced mountaineers.

Visualization: *This section of switchbacks allows you to go into*

> **CAUTION**
>
> **Just because someone suggested you take an ice ax and crampons, these items are of little or no value—even harmful—if you don't have the skill or experience in using them.** *Unless you already own the proper equipment, have used it, and know how to self-arrest, you are better off to turn back at this point. If the switchbacks are covered with snow, the trip is no longer a "hike"—it's full winter mountaineering.*

the coast mode—just moving along effortlessly, breathing deeply and exhaling with pressure. Looking along the Trail for Sky Pilot and Sierra Golds, you are impressed with your own innate ability to prepare for this experience. You have hydrated with just the right amount of liquids. You have eaten just the proper kinds and amounts of food for the trip. Your shoes are the very best choice, and your clothing is keeping your body at the perfect temperature. With very little effort, you arrive at Trail Crest.

Trail Crest: 8.5 mi., 13,645 feet el.

When you get to Trail Crest, you have reached the summit, for all intents and purposes. You can look over the ridge and feast your eyes on the vastness beyond—the headwaters of the Kern River, and many peaks and valleys of the Western Sierra. You have attained an altitude just short of that at The Top, and your efforts are well rewarded by the magnificent view. A sign marks the dividing line between Inyo National Forest and Sequoia National Park. You now enter the National Park system (leaving behind the National Forest Service), which is run by a different part of the U.S. Government, and patrolled by a different set of Rangers.

> *"Superbe et Grandiose"*
> - **PARIS, FRANCE**

Visualization: *Now you have the 360-degree view of the world below at*

13,645' elevation. Look to the west and see the grand vistas of lakes, meadows, and ridge lines. Turning south, you marvel at Discovery Pinnacles, Arc Pass, and the Cottonwood Lakes area. As you move along, the summit of Whitney appears. Your route will be downhill now for a little while, and the Trail becomes rocky and more uneven. But, knowing how well you have done this far, you will move forward with ease, always taking the right step and feeling secure as you progress toward your goal.

John Muir Trail Junction: 9.0 miles, 13,480 feel el.

After reaching Trail Crest, you will come upon a welcome downhill stretch which takes you to a fork in the Trail. (This is the "dreaded" uphill on the return trip.) To the left is the route to Crabtree Meadow, down the "back side" of Whitney. To the right is the final approach to the summit. Either way you turn, you are now on the famous John Muir Trail.

__Visualization:__ The summit and the hut are in view now. As you walk along the west side of the ridge, the Trail becomes more rugged, with short ups and downs, a narrow pathway, and uneven steps. Ahead you will pass the John Muir Trail fork that heads to Yosemite. Make a mental note of this site because as the hikers come up from the west (Guitar Lake, Crabtree Meadow), most will leave their packs around the signs or group in the area for a break.

NOTE: ON YOUR WAY BACK from the summit, be sure you turn left—the "dreaded" uphill—to come over Trail Crest and retrace your steps down the Whitney Trail. REMEMBER as you come back from the summit, the return trail to HOME—Whitney Portal (on the east side of the mountain), your car, the road, all of these important things, are on the Trail that heads UP to get down. Every year we have people who take the wrong direction, which sometimes leads to a rescue operation. Make a little song, "Sometimes I got to go up to get down."

The sign was corrected at the JMT Junction several years ago, but we still have people take the JMT west on the way down. During the 2017 season, a rescue was made for a stranded hiker who had originally been leading a group. He argued he knew the way down, but his group took the correct descent trail instead of following him. He was rescued a day later at Crabtree Meadow (potential for recovery).

A short distance down from the junction, there are some tent sites where adventurers may decide to camp. Waking up to a sunrise here is a very memorable experience, but plan ahead for a cold night and for your water needs. Be sure you are carrying enough; there is no reliable source along this section.

The Trail along the west side of the ridge to the final peak is another "photo opportunity" for marvelous views in every direction. Between the Needles, you can look eastward down upon Lone Pine, and across Owens Valley to the Inyo Mountains beyond. With a turn of the head, you can see the Kaweahs towering on the other side, and the deep trench of Kern Canyon. Looking closer, you will easily identify Guitar Lake below (it is shaped like a guitar), and various peaks to the north and south.

Because of the high altitude, hiking the last two miles to the summit can be taxing, even though the Trail is not steep. Your mental acuity may decrease due to lack of oxygen to the brain. Headaches are common, as well as nausea. Like morning sickness, this is best treated by eating a small snack. Drink water, even if you don't feel thirsty. If symptoms increase, be aware that you will not get better until you GO BACK DOWN TO A LOWER ELEVATION. If you begin vomiting, your body is losing too much liquid. The only cure for altitude sickness is to GET DOWN.

We should mention the various landmarks along this final ascent. Mt. Muir, elevation 14,015, rises to the right a short distance from the fork in the Trail. A mile further, Crooks Peak and Keeler Needle can be seen to the right. There is one particularly exposed point along here where both sides of the Trail drop off steeply. Anyone who suffers from the fear of

"Sleeping on Mt. Whitney was the greatest night of my life"
- UK FORCES, GERMANY

heights (acrophobia) should not attempt this trail.

As you near the summit, you will meet people coming down. Many of them will encourage you—just as others encouraged them. You are almost there!

Visualization: Moving along now, the summit is only 1.9 miles from the John Muir Junction. The last little area of confusion is just below the summit. The Trail may be hard to follow due to false trails, snow patches, and rockslides covering it for short sections. Look left along the same contour you are standing on, and the Trail is on this contour for several hundred feet. Then switchbacks lead up to the summit area. About ten minutes will take you through this area and then the hut is visible. No one can stop you now!

Summit: 11 miles, 14,508 more or less.

What can we say about the summit that has not already been said? Sign the register; catch your breath; rest awhile; exchange a high five or two; eat your trail mix; take lots of photos; enjoy the jets if they fly by; try identifying all the surrounding peaks; and get out of there by 5:00 p.m. if you are planning to go all the way down today. You still have a long hike ahead of you, and you must reach Lone Pine Lake by nightfall.

On the other hand, you may be planning to sleep at the summit. This can be hazardous—storms are unpredictable and lightning is a fatal force. However, if you are prepared, and the weather is good, go for it—set up camp and get acquainted with any others who have the same plan. We know of a group of over 15 backpackers who camped on the summit to celebrate the 85th birthday of one in their party. It was his eleventh climb. They even had a birthday cake! His wife participated by hiring a plane and flying over the top.

Going Down

Let's go over the hardest part of the trip: "going down." All of the things most people do are focused on getting to the top. Well, that's exactly half way. At the top you will notice your feet and hands have swollen, your socks are wet, your lips are chapped, and your bottom is covered with heat rash. Your feet will be slammed into the end of your boots on the way down, leaving your big toes very sore. Your shoulders are raw from an overloaded pack, and half the gear you bought is in some kind of disrepair or lost. Your eyes are red, and exposed skin like the tops of your ears, your nose, the back of your neck, and your legs are sunburned. You are tired and just want it to be over.

The Trail takes on a different persona going down. You are now resisting motion downward and forward. As you move along the trail, the solid placement of footing and pressure loading is turned into quick front foot placement and pushing off with the other leg on smooth even sections. This is great, but from the summit to Outpost Camp that doesn't exist. What you have is uneven, rocky, slick, gravel-covered trail that is driving you forward. You now have to think about every step's placement: Is it solid, not tilting or slanting, and stable so that as you lift the other leg will the footing hold?

We cannot emphasize enough that reaching the summit is only half the battle. The hike down uses a whole different set of muscles, and holds its own potential for disaster. Folks coming down are usually fatigued, careless, and thus more susceptible to falls. They may not be disciplined about staying with their party. This can result in the problems of separation, miscommunication, misunderstanding, and an unnecessary call to the Sheriff's Search and Rescue Operations.

We see many people leave the summit and travel too far down the back side. Then when all the false trails run out, they see people along the Trail and have to climb up to join it. As sunlight diminishes, it becomes more difficult to stay on the Trail and avoid accidents. With the dark comes the cold, the risk of hypothermia, and the formation of ice on the wet areas of the trail.

Walking sticks and ski poles play

"Thanks for the poles! Wouldn't have made it without them"
- SAN DIEGO, CA

"I swear it is farther coming down than going up"
- SHINGLE SPRINGS, CA

a very big role in balance and allowing one to take the shock off feet, ankles, knees, and lower body by placing an extended pole in front of you and steadying yourself with it as you gently place your foot. Most people who use trekking poles say that coming down without them would have been a lot worse. Some even tell us they couldn't have made it down without them.

Should you buy them? That's your decision, but you should never pass the chance to rent them or borrow them. We take them on every trip, and when one of us goes up to help someone down, we will not leave until we find an extra pair. These people who need help are generally exhausted, and usually have a problem with feet, ankles, or knees, and are moving slowly. Offering them the poles, and taking their packs, we can usually get them to walk to the Portal.

Stay together as you make your descent. This could save your life, or someone else's. Be aware of what is happening around you and be willing to give help where needed. You got yourself up the mountain and you are expected to get yourself down. If someone is in trouble, don't pass them by—find out what is wrong and make it right if you can.

Some people think they are doing someone in trouble a favor by hurrying past them to report the problem to the Store. This causes a longer delay in getting help than if the "message bearer" would have just given the needed help, sending someone else down with a report.

Another problem people have coming down is their loss of focus. They are thinking, "It's over, it's easy going downhill." Well, for many people, it's about the same amount of time coming down as going up, because of fatigue. Experienced hikers will come down faster than first-timers. The majority of accidents happen on the way down due to dehydration, exhaustion, and hypothermia. Look around and take in the view you may have missed on the way up. Talk with hikers going up. Do a little investigation on how they really look. What is their skin color, how are their eyes, speech, spirit level, pack size, shoes, and gear? File this away for your next experience. What we have learned is, "Everybody has the right stuff." By noticing what seems to work and what doesn't, you can save yourself some trial and error.

On the way down, look for short goals to reach. "When I get to ___, I will have a snack. I will look at the waterfall, take a picture of Mirror Lake from above, etc." Chances are you will only do this once, and your experience on film and/or stored in the big database you are equipped with should be loaded.

From Outpost Camp to the Portal, the Trail is somewhat forgiving. It is mostly dirt and easy to follow. If evening sets in, you should be OK the rest of the way down. You can see the lights of Lone Pine show up, and watch the headlights of cars going up and down the Portal Road.

When traveling in a group, one person should have a light focused on the trail. Head lamps can be a novelty item, when you purchase the most expensive one you can find, show it to the group and leave it in the car. Six people with 100-300-lumen lights moving nonstop for 4-6 hours will drive you crazy or may cause vertigo. Think of the bouncing ball on the old black and white movies. A light held in your hand can be somewhat controlled, and you can find a light that will last many hours longer.

Watch for the stream crossing at North Fork of Lone Pine Creek—it can be crossed by walking through the water (We have gone to this area a number of times to help people cross in the dark.) After this crossing, the parking lot and campground appear. Now you have the chance to look up the canyon and see the hiker's flashlights coming down. Many nights this will go on until early morning, and about 2:00-3:00 a.m. the early starters will head upward. Once we asked a group why they wanted to start so early. Their response was, they didn't want to walk in the dark.

Let's talk about changes as we age. We tend to slow down, have problems with balance and are a little less agile. We cannot focus as well on the terrain depending on prescription problems with glasses or those GD sunglasses

> "Biggest pile of rocks I've ever seen!"
> - BAKERSFIELD, CA

> "Come to Colorado—there are all kinds of rock piles"
> - DENVER, CO

in the dark. I do not think age is a factor in summiting, but take caution about physical/mental adjustments. Older hikers do very well; many have years of experience. They have worked out a system of gear and a pace they like to travel, and most often outgrow that ego problem (potential for recovery).

Trailhead: 22 miles, 8,367 feet el.

Congratulations—you made it! Now you can celebrate—treat yourself to whatever luxury you've been thinking about (hot shower, cold drink, fresh food, etc.). When you get home, please take the time to record and post your trip at www.mountwhitney forum.com. The Store's message board has become a busy place where you can share your experience and your photos.

A welcome sight for most.

Yet Another Success Story—Here is a note dropped off after a one-day hike some years ago:

> **To the Portal Store Family:**
> Thank you so very much for providing me with the absolute best advice on climbing "The Big One," especially in one day.
> Your book was the best book out of the many I read before arriving to the Portal.
> I loved reading about the history—from the naming of Mt. Whitney, to the trails, to the cabins, to the history of your precious store—all of it written as if we were outside, enjoying a cold beer, and you were talking to me from across the table. At the summit, I wrote, "Thank you Mr. Gustave!" I wouldn't have had the appreciation of his work if I'd not read your book.
> I followed your advice; I truly did! It not only helped me recognize when a member of our group needed to get back down (he couldn't recite the alphabet and that's when he, too, realized it was time to turn around), but it also helped me make sure the others were constantly eating and drinking and stopping for a minute or two to take in the beauty of the climb. Without your constant reminder that one must respect our body's signals, Mike could have been in real danger and the others may have never made it. Thank you.
> But, the best advice you gave me was to enjoy the experience by never breaking a sweat and never getting out of breath. I honestly made it to the top (8:30) feeling fresh, and of course, elated! I followed your advice and it worked.
> While we chatted afterwards, many of my motley crew asked me about other trails, the cabins, bears, the history—with every question, I opened up your book, turned to page "x" and gave them the answer. You won't be surprised when I tell you one of them said, "I should have read that book." I told him he could have my copy for "next time."
> Hope to see you again.

A climber carefully working their way up the Mountaineeer's Route

THE MOUNTAINEER'S ROUTE

The Mountaineer's Route is an alternate way to the summit that can be climbed without special equipment by experienced mountaineers. John Muir was the first to find this way up, which is a shorter, more direct route than the Trail, but is also steeper and more challenging.

We added a Guide for the Mountaineer's Route in the 2nd edition, with a caveat to those who are not ready for it: If an inexperienced hiker attempts the Mountaineer's Route, they are setting themselves up for failure (potential for recovery).

Over the years some people are using some of the old routes in the first canyon, and on the downclimb taking a dead-end route into the willows after the ledges. A very experienced climber may do well and get up or down but at the end of the day only does more resource damage, makes a false system of trails to nowhere, and has and can cause accidents. So, I suggest you follow the established climber's path, remove false cairns as you find them, and help protect the area by removing small stones as you walk. If you see someone off the trail, offer to guide them back onto the established route.

We also see many take the false trails out of the Lower Boy Scout Lake area. As you come to Lower Boy Scout Lake, STOP and look to the south along the edge of the Meadow. You will see a path that stays low; follow the lower path.

Why You Shouldn't Go If You Aren't Ready

It has been our observation that inexperienced hikers who try to climb the Mountaineer's Route start up and get stuck. They thrash around in the drainage, trying to find their way, and do a lot of damage to the area. This

> "Mountaineer's Route— Yowza!"
> - DANVILLE, CA

> "Such Granite!"
> - CHATSWORTH, CA

results in heavy impact on the local wilderness resources. The water, plants, soil, and animals exist in a delicate balance which is easily upset.

This beautiful canyon, in its purest, undisturbed natural form, could yield a truer "Mt. Whitney Experience" than the heavily-traveled Trail, for those who have the skills to enjoy it. It is unfortunate that it has been treated with disrespect by some and is no longer a pristine area. As John Muir said, this Route is for those with "well-seasoned limbs." His term for the Whitney Trail was the "mule way."

Here are some suggestions for those who are interested in this version of the Whitney Experience and feel they are ready:

- Be aware that this is not a designated trail. It is an established climber's path leading up the North Fork drainage of Lone Pine Creek.
- Just because permits are sometimes available for this route, don't assume that "just anyone" should attempt it. If you aren't able to get a permit for the Whitney Trail, do not use this as a rationale for obtaining a permit for the Mountaineer's Route.
- If you are not an experienced mountaineer with map-reading skills, or able to follow a "climbers trail," don't try it. This Route requires full mountaineering skills.
- If you feel you are ready to try it, consider hiring a guide for your first trip up. We have names of professionals who will help you succeed. The Forest Service Supervisors Office in Bishop is another good source for names of qualified guides.
- If you cannot afford a guide, put up a sign on the bulletin board at your local sporting goods store asking for a climbing partner who knows the Route. You can also post a request on various websites, including our message board at www.mountwhitneyforum.com.

- Be careful selecting a partner. Do several warm-up hikes to test each other's comfort level and skill level.
- There are other published Guides available for the Mountaineer's Route. While we realize the authors' intent is good, and they know the Route themselves, it can be deceptive to lead a person up this canyon who is not capable of climbing it.
- Many sources imply some type of easy ingress to the area by a few simple photos. After numerous excursions up this canyon, we have concluded that the most deceptive part of this Route is its severity.
- An experienced mountaineer will do just as well or better with a topo map than with written instructions and photos which can easily be misinterpreted.

Description

This route, although only 3.4 miles one way, rises 6,000 feet above the Portal, at some points is a class three climb if you know the exact route (but can move quickly into class 5 if you don't know where you're going), and IS NOT FOR THE FAINT OF HEART! Again, this is NOT a trail. The route should be easy to follow for experienced climbers. If all of us would use the same path, it would stop the severe damage being perpetrated in this drainage by tramping around on false routes. The path you follow has been used for a long time by mountaineers. Stay on the main route that has been plainly marked. We could talk about cairns/ducks, but we know that all schools of thought will never agree as to what's right. Our opinion: if they are wrong take them down, but if they mark critical points, leave them.

Also, as climbers we should set the example of taking out our own trash and human waste. Before you go, make sure you pick up a WAG Bag at the Store or the Ranger Station. On the

"I swam in Iceberg Lake!"
- MANHATTAN BEACH, CA

"Jan got a little beat up on the chute. Search and Rescue saved the day! Thanks"
- LOS ANGELES, CA

way out, you can dispose of used bags in the covered can at the trailhead at the Portal.

Take the main Whitney Trail to the North Fork of Lone Pine Creek sign. This is 150 feet before you reach the John Muir Wilderness Boundary sign. If you have any doubt, stay on the Whitney Trail to the Wilderness sign and then come back down the Trail 150 feet, re-crossing the Creek. Next, turn around so you're facing up the Trail, and head up to your RIGHT on the NORTH SIDE of the North Fork Creek. About 200 feet up this path you may see a sign, "Mountaineer's Route." (The sign for Mountaineer's Route will often go missing.)

Follow this path up through the trees and ferns until it flattens out. This will be about a quarter of the way up the canyon. From here you should see the notch/gap below Lower Boy Scout Lake. Continue on about 100 feet and you will cross to the south side of the stream. There will be somewhat of a tunnel through the willows exiting onto a slab (10' rock).

Follow the path up the south side, below the wall and above the stream. As the canyon narrows down and the path joins the slabs, you will re-cross the stream to the north side. This crossing can be very wet and icy. The stream has two threads at this point. Boulder hop across the first stream of water until you reach a mud slope (about 15 feet). If a log is standing there, avoid it and climb up the mud slope. About 20 feet more will take you to the next crossing, where you'll go down and rock-hop again and cross next to or under a waterfall. Avoid the slick log lying in the water.

As you leave the water, go to the wall and turn up the canyon. Fifty feet along the base of the wall will take you to a dead end. This is the start of the Ebersbacher Ledges. Look up and to the right, and you will see the "pine tree." Work your way up the crack to the tree. Continue above the trees to the wall, then look to the east and the ramp is straight ahead. Stay close to the wall and you should see the path. Walk 150' east on this narrow ramp (level). At this point you will step up, gaining about three feet of elevation. Follow this ramp, continuing east for 175 feet, staying next to the wall (away from the drop-off). This will get you to a short section of stair steps about 5 feet up and about 5 feet east.

MAKE A MENTAL NOTE OF THIS POINT. This is the turning point on the way down. If you miss this and continue on the upper ledge, you will need rope and climbing skills to get down.

As you leave the ledge, head straight for the main wall in front of you. At the base of this wall (100') you will find the path. Follow the path at the base of the wall until it exits onto an open area, and you will see the notch/gap below Lower Boy Scout Lake. From here, the path is easy to follow.

At the notch, lose a little elevation and you will see a clearing on your left to cross over the outlet for Lower Boy Scout Lake. NEVER go up the scree slope. Stay along the vegetation line as you travel past Lower Boy Scout Lake. Cross here to the south side and follow the path through the trees to the boulder field. Look along the base of the left scree slope (left or south side of Lower Boy Scout Lake). You will see the track to follow to the west. Also, you'll see two giant rocks near the waterfall. You will begin climbing here. Head to the downhill side of the lower boulder. Stay close to this rock. As you get to the rock you will see the willows. At the very edge of the downhill side of the lower rock is the path. Follow it into the willows about 15' and it will turn north on a slab and down into a small stream. Cross this stream, work up several feet, and cross another thread of water. You will be to the right of the stream.

As you exit this crossing you will be at a slab. Climb onto the slab and follow it to a group of trees (approximately 1,500' distance). These slabs will be icy and very slick—if not icy, mossy, so watch your step at all times through this section.

CAUTION: When you get near Clyde Meadow, do not go into the closed bowl of Upper Boy Scout Lake. Make sure you travel in a southerly curve around the ridge. When you get to the trees (Clyde Meadow), look up and left to the gap/saddle and follow slabs to the path that switchbacks up to this saddle. You will find a grand path at this point.

Now that you are here at 11,500'+ elevation, let's talk it over. You have never had to use any more than walking skills. You are about halfway up, and your last water spot is Iceberg Lake which is just above you. Turn around, look to the east, and enjoy the view of the North Fork Drainage. Your line of sight should be almost a straight path to the Portal.

Ascend past the small water-seep below Iceberg Lake. Many old climbers used the west end of the water-seep to climb up to Iceberg Lake, but now most people travel past the water (at certain times of the year it may be a wide waterfall) and go up the next draw to the west. This route is much safer and faster with a pack. It takes you to Iceberg Lake.

The Mountaineer's Route takes the gully to the notch at 14,000'. Several ways will get you to the notch. We suggest taking the left chute just south of the main gully. However, this depends on snow or ice conditions and your skill level. If you take the main chute, rockfall and people in the chute above make it worth staying to the right or left as much as you can. Also, in the middle of the main chute there is a large boulder blocking the path. Don't climb up to it and try climbing around it. Pick a course around it about 50' below and it's fairly easy. The chute above this point is about 45 degrees, and below is about 40 degrees.

From the notch, several choices exist. The traditional Mountaineer's Route follows the first chute to the south. Another choice, the "easy walk off," is never easy. It's exceptionally risky if there's snow and ice on this traverse. This is a 50+ degree slope for about a quarter mile. Full climbing gear with ice skills and tools are needed. On the other hand, if studied, the first chute to the south of the notch will reveal a path up on rock for most of the summer. Again, this will require climbing skills, and a lot of people turn back at the notch. During the 2017 season "the easy walk off" had the tenth (actual recovery).

The last several hundred feet is not that important. The exposure picks up in this section and is a factor to consider on the way down if you continue up. Some people choose to walk down the Whitney Trail after summiting, making it a circle trip.

Thoughts from Doug Sr.:

One day I was talking to a guy about the Mountaineer's Route and how it tends to attract hikers who have been up the Trail several times, and for something different they want to go up the

Mountaineer's Route. Or, the really skilled mathematicians who deduct that this route is only 3.4 miles (versus 11 miles) decide to try it. Others notice that there are guidebooks for sale that describe the area "to a fashion." These writeups don't include much detail, not wanting to cheat you out of the "discovery" experience that most mountaineers enjoy and expect. But then again, most mountaineers would not buy a book or trust these flowery dream-walk descriptions.

Now to the point—as we were chatting, a young woman came to the counter with four tootsie roll pops and three candy bars. She said that last year she and her friend went up Langley and the next hike planned was Whitney. She needed to get home, so her friend did the Mountaineer's Route by himself and took a fatal fall on the "easy walk off" section.

Most people who write these descriptions have very little chance to see how critical good information is. What may have looked good in a drought year can turn into a sheet of blue ice for the next two seasons, and at this Whitney place, skill levels are a little short of the ego. Climbers at times show bad judgement on the way down the Mountaineer's Route. One day I was going up the last section and noticed two climbers coming down into an ice flow, and I asked if they had a new way down. One admitted they had just soloed the East Face and were clueless as to how to get down. This didn't stop them from starting down with no idea where to go. We have a term for this now, EEA (Ego Exceeds Ability).

Another aspect of this North Fork route is that each storm can change the condition and characteristics. What may be ice and snow one week can turn to waist deep snow that takes hours to travel a mile in. Iceberg Lake can stay frozen until mid-July, and certain parts of the chute will remain snow covered year-round.

> "You don't get your permits at the trailhead— we found out the hard way and had to drive all the way back to town!"
> - SANTA BARBARA, CA

"Though SAR teams will do everything possible to assist you, YOU ARE NOT GUARANTEED A RESCUE."
(Photos by Bob Rockwell)

WHEN SOMETHING GOES WRONG

Tied Down: Can you leave one of your party midway up the chute, between Iceberg and the notch? Well, yes, if you tie them down it seems (actual recovery).

When we hear, "I left my friends," we can now finish the story and know most likely it will involve car keys or "I don't have a ride to town" or "They should be down later, but could you start a rescue?" Given that no one is hurt, and there is no clue where they are or at which camp they may have decided to spend the night—or if they have walked off the trail—it's what leads to, "I heard someone yelling for help..."

A group of three couples ordered food. Earlene took the order and I went back to start cooking. Thinking one of the ladies said she heard someone yelling for help, her husband said, "No, it didn't sound like real, 'Help!'." I go out to the table and ask the lady where she heard the yelling. She gave me enough information that I knew someone had missed the trail, gone down to Lone Pine Lake and followed the drainage until they cliffed out. This area is about 300' south of the Whitney Trail and is one of the "traps" people get into.

I grabbed my phone, poles, bag and went up. I found the person and walked him to the trail; he was fine. I then went down and had a nice conversation with the group of six. Do you help when you hear, "Help!"? Or do you ignore helping and keep it inside, never bringing it up to anyone else?

What do you think?

Different day, same drill, not only did they hear, "Help!" but had pictures of the area. That very smart, handsome young Myles was working that day. We called Search and Rescue, and then took the cross-country route

"We climbed the Rock— and lived!"
- **CULVER CITY, CA**

"It was hell and heaven put together!"
- **SAN FERNANDO VALLEY, CA**

to the pictured area (Same location as the above-mentioned story). About 100' from the base of the cliff, I asked Myles if he was up to the problem, if the fall had been fatal or worst-case broken up and bleeding out; he was solid. We found one person at the bottom of the 100' cliff and another on top of the cliff that looked like the old deer in the headlights—not taking another step. The person at the bottom was very lucky; he was injured but not seriously. Myles walked the other person down and guided Search and Rescue to the location.

Some interesting observations: the person at the bottom stated, "I can't move or walk," yet we found tracks all around the area at the bottom where someone had moved the pack, placed a sleeping pad down on a level area, and left footprints to the stream several times for water. You see a lot sometimes.

The Saturday Night Special

The Store owners use this expression—The Saturday Night Special (and Sunday, Monday...)—to describe a phenomenon that has become almost as predictable as Old Faithful during peak season. Business is winding down after a crowded, crazy day. We are tired, but we know it's Saturday night, and the fun isn't over yet.

Inevitably, someone comes in around sundown to report their friend or relative is lost on the Mountain. The person is beginning to panic because they suddenly realize the potential for disaster as night sets in. They may have been up and down parts of the Trail several times searching for the missing person. Why does this happen? What can be done about it?

Traffic on the Whitney Trail peaks over the weekend. Hikers take off work early on Friday, drive up to the Portal, and head up the Trail on Saturday morning. The majority of them have not taken the time to study and prepare for the trek. They envision a quick "mountain high" over the weekend, and do not think ahead, or discuss all the potential scenarios with their partners.

If a party consists of more than two people, they may not feel any need to stay together. The faster climbers might go ahead while the rest of the group sets a slower pace, planning to meet at the summit. Any number of things can happen to cause a missed connection. Slower hikers will not reach the summit in one day and may decide to turn back. Adventurous climbers may stray off the Trail to capture a particular view on film or examine a cluster of wildflowers more closely. The net result is, the sun goes down without everyone knowing where everyone else is. Suddenly they want help.

What should you do if someone in your group is missing? Spread the word, and look for them in an organized fashion; if not successful, get help. When? The answer depends on a number of factors: age of the person (elderly, a child, or neither); their physical and mental condition; their clothing and gear; the weather, location, time of day; and more.

Another common case of The Saturday Night Special occurs with a couple when one person has trouble getting down, and the other leaves to come down for help. The irony in this situation is that if you leave your friend in trouble on the mountain alone, you have just deprived him or her of the best help available—your own presence. Most people have more ability to help their friends overcome adversity than they realize. If your friend is developing hypothermia, give up your extra jacket. Put your arms around him or her. Do some jumping jacks together and get their body temperature up.

If someone in your party is suffering from altitude sickness and/or dehydration, the worst thing you can do is leave that person on the trail. If someone is weak, take that person's pack for a while and help them get to a lower altitude. Remember the song, "Lean on Me." If someone is feeling faint, offer some water and keep up the encouragement. Leaving someone alone on the mountain in a weakened condition is a life-threatening choice. **THINK CAREFULLY** before you do it. No one else can make the decision.

> "...the rescue, which took many hours, required 11 volunteer SAR members and a California Highway Patrol helicopter flying in dicey high-wind conditions.
> ...five people fell in a matter of minutes.
> ...[other] hikers...sat vigil for hours, wrapping the victims in sleeping bags and checking their vitals."
>
> - MEGAN MICHELSON, OUTSIDE MAGAZINE, AUG 9, 2018

YOU have to choose, based on the situation. If you must separate (i.e. broken bones, can't walk) make sure they have extra clothes, shelter, food, water, and if possible, some company. Most hikers are kindly people, and like to help if they can. The problem is that our society has numbed a lot of people's initiative, so they don't realize they can help unless someone else makes the suggestion. Use your imagination. Use your sense of self-reliance. Take charge and show you care—it may save a life.

In case of injury, the reporting party should have as much information as possible about the hiker in trouble: name, age, where from, current location, injuries, pulse rate, degree of mobility, level of protective clothing, color of clothing, and general condition (vomiting, shaking, pale, bleeding, etc.).

When we are faced with The Saturday Night Special, we have the unpleasant job of telling the distraught hiker some bad news. First, rescue efforts made during the night are on foot only, since landing a helicopter on the Mountain after sundown is limited. Second, the Sheriff's Department must evaluate the situation first and determine whether or not to call out the Volunteer Search Party. Third, a few pointed questions often bring the person to the unpleasant realization that they could have, and should have, taken care of the problem themselves.

Rescues

It must be made clear that THERE ARE NO RESCUE CAPABILITIES AT THE PORTAL. Many visitors to this area do not understand the concept of "Wilderness." This has led to many troublesome confrontations with distraught party members about the lack of instantaneous resolution to emergency needs.

Many people have misconceptions about the process of initiating, organizing, and conducting a rescue. A number of different agencies and organizations are available to perform rescue operations, but there are limitations on what can be done, depending on the time of day and the seriousness of an incident.

When an injury is reported, the Sheriff's Department is contacted and given all information available. If they determine that an injury is minor, and night has fallen, the most likely course of action is to notify a volunteer search organization to mobilize for an early morning start if the party does not come down under his/her own power.

If an injury is significant to the degree that the person is immobilized, a Command Post is set up and several search party members are dispatched to the location with medical and/or survival equipment. A Command Post is a temporary communications system that connects a station on the Whitney Portal Road with the airport, the Sheriff's station, and those on the mountain conducting the search and rescue.

The "best case" scenario is when someone with the injured party is able to locate a Ranger on the Trail. Ideally, the Ranger would have radio contact with the Ranger Station or Dispatch in Lone Pine and would report the problem. That Station would in turn call the Sheriff's Department to dispatch any available rescue unit. It should be emphasized that this chain of events happens very seldom due to limited Ranger contact, and the low probability that a helicopter will be available immediately. Also, most accidents do not happen during ideal conditions. People tend to get hurt during inclement weather, and often it is after sundown. This means there is high wind, overcast skies, and darkness—conditions making it impossible to fly into the area.

Both military and contract helicopters are used for rescues on Mt. Whitney. The Navy, the Highway Patrol, National Parks, and the Forest Service are all called upon to conduct helicopter rescue operations, depending on season and availability. Privately owned helicopters are contracted out of Independence by the Forest Service for firefighting operations during the summer months. If not out fighting a fire, they may be called upon for Search and Rescue duties. When a helicopter is not available in Independence, the Sheriff's Department may call the California Highway Patrol (CHP) to dispatch a crew from as far

> "Traveling in the wilderness presents risks. Rescues can be costly, dangerous, and difficult. Though SAR teams will do everything possible to assist you, YOU ARE NOT GUARANTEED A RESCUE."
>
> – INYO COUNTY SEARCH AND RESCUE

away as Fresno. Navy helicopters are another option, and may be dispatched from Lemoore Naval Air Station, China Lake, or Travis Air Force Base. When a hiker is in trouble on the west side of Mt. Whitney, the National Park Service Rangers may call air rescue teams from Kings Canyon or Sequoia. Because of these various resources and the distances involved, there is a wide range in the time it may take for a rescue unit to arrive after a call for help has been made.

What does a Search and Rescue (SAR) helicopter ride cost? Emergency transport from Whitney to Lone Pine is provided as a public service (no charge). If the party needs to be flown out of the area, the cost will be in the thousands of dollars.

The shortest amount of time we have ever seen between an injury and a subsequent rescue is about two hours. Most rescues take six to eight hours. Some may take from twelve hours to several days.

Rescues on Mt. Whitney are not like on TV or in a movie, where help appears to be immediate. Some visitors to the area have suggested that since they paid for their "ticket" to hike the Trail (a permit), they should have access to instant rescue capabilities with all the modern devices and apparatus available in a big city. What they don't understand is that the Wilderness Act specifies a limitation on mechanized vehicles. There is a fine line and some differences of opinion about whether a rescue helicopter is in violation by going into a Wilderness Area.

It has been argued, from a climber's standpoint, that you cheat people out of an experience by rescuing them. A full mountain experience includes an acceptance of the "ride," and people should be obligated to help themselves. No one should be expected to violate this code by bringing in special equipment. The only proper resource for someone in trouble should be other climbers who come to help.

What Happens at The Store

While there are no established rescue capabilities at the Portal, we who have spent time behind the counter know the terrible outcome if someone is left unattended with a minor injury and not taken care of for shock or hypothermia. As we listen to the details being related to us, we are mentally calculating the hours of exposure that have already occurred, and how many more hours it will take for a rescue operation to reach the person. Unfortunately, there are occasions when we realize that the clock has run out.

WHAT WE DO AT THE STORE:

1. **Call the Inyo County Sheriff's dispatch** at 760-878-0383, rather than 911. A call from a cell phone to 911 connects with the CHP, and we have had trouble with communications. For problems over the crest, Sequoia/Kings is called at 209-565-3195.

2. **Gather all details:** who, what, where, and when.

3. **Find out if the party is moving**, and if so, which direction (up or down?). Also, consider if they could have made a wrong turn at Trail Crest. Has anybody seen them on "this side" of the mountain? If not, they may be on the west side.

4. **Figure out which trail they are on.** Which canyon are they in? Where did they start, and how did it look? We can usually tell if they started up the "true" or "false" (Carillon Drainage) Mountaineer's Route, or most other canyons, if someone can give a description of the terrain.

5. **Receive a call back from a Sheriff,** who will talk with the reporting party. They may dispatch a Sheriff to come to the Portal Store for a report and evaluation.

6. **Talk to hikers coming in off the Trail** to gather news. When we have information such as the color of the person's hat or pack, their gender, age, etc., we can piece together a running report of where and when the person was seen, and how they were doing. This is VERY CRITICAL information. It helps the Sheriff determine whether they are moving, and how fast. Figuring out how long it took them to get from point A to point

> "The goal should not be the Whitney summit - the goal is to safely return to the Portal parking lot."
> - MESSAGE BOARD

B will give important clues about where they are now (point C). Many times, the person in trouble walks out before rescue arrives. During the busy part of the season we will put out a sign at the trailhead saying, if you are with a party that has requested a rescue and you no longer need a rescue, please call the dispatch and cancel the rescue.

    7. **Submit a report to the Sheriff,** who can then radio for help if determined appropriate, as described above. Next comes the long wait for a search party and/or helicopter to be mobilized.

What do we do in the meantime?

Father and son (Doug Sr. and Jr.) have a 2-1/2-mile limit. If we can help, we leave the Store, grab a day pack with supplies, and go. If someone is tired, blistered, beat up from a fall, or has an ankle or knee injury, and they are moving, we take their pack. We give them water, ice, candy, two walking sticks, and talk to them.

Once we went up and a couple was having trouble getting down because his wife had hurt her ankle. The husband would carry her down several hundred feet on his back, leave her on a rock, and then go back and bring down their packs. This was easy to help with; we just took their packs, and everyone got down in no time.

We had the only communication system in the Portal area for at least 10 years. We used a radio/phone system and called in many rescues and emergency calls. Now, many times we will call to follow up and confirm a call was received or understood from someone reporting from the mountain. We also have a base station that links to agencies on the command base so that Search and Rescue can talk with the ranger/fire crew/dispatch/Forest Service and County.

Many years ago, a young man came in and reported two of his group were stranded on a cliff. We placed a call and I asked the young man if he would like to show me where they went off trail. After a short hike we were at the start of the cross-country route. We then returned to the Store where I gave an update to the dispatcher. I went back up to the North Fork area, met with the back-country ranger, and we located the stranded climbers. Using my cell phone, I contacted Earlene. She replied, "the sheriff is here for details." The sheriff was not from the area, and dispatch was not familiar with the local area names. I went back down and got a climbing rope. I went back up the North Fork and placed the rope on the face that would get to the cliffed-out climbers. The ranger and I tried to down climb from above, but darkness set in and we had to return to the Portal. The next morning the two climbers were lowered down.

Recall that survey stuff? (See Intro to 3rd edition.) We needed a way to take the information from the reporting party to locate the area where the event occurred, give that location to dispatch, and then to the unit that responds. We created a basic topo map with a grid overlay and a system that broke the grid into sub grids. For example, a topo with 32 squares, then an overlay broken into 4 sub squares A, B, C, and D. That again is broken into 4 sub squares 1, 2, 3, and 4. As an example, a person walks in and says, "My buddy fell." We take out the map and ask if he can point out the area or tell us how it looks. We see it is in the big square #18, upper left side—that is "D," and his finger is on the lower right side of "D" so that is 2. Now we have a position within 500 feet: "18-D-2." This we can give to the dispatch and they can turn it into UTM (Universal Transverse Mercator) coordinates. The stranded climbers were very strong but not great at map reading. Ego and peer pressure climbed them into trouble (potential for recovery).

The fly-by and the Canadians

One of the first things Search and Rescue does is a helicopter fly-by. One winter, they flew by a climber on the face. Weather was coming in, with high wind gusts and failing light. The plan was to locate the climber and do a ground rescue. The next morning the climber was located, but he didn't survive the night.

Some years later, a young man came into the store and said his friend took a fall on the East Face. He couldn't help so I did the drill; we called Search and Rescue and yes, let's get back up there and bring a sleeping bag, a climbing rack and another rope. Dispatch calls back and says to wait for the "Fast" team. Three

A Portal bear taking a stroll

hours go by and still no "Fast" team. Now it's 4:30, the sunlight is fading, and a storm is moving in. We called back and were told the team is on the way and to wait. Soon it was 7:30-8:00 p.m., no team. About 8:30 the first team shows up, but the plan is to go up the Whitney Trail, 10 miles vs. 4 miles. The team starts up the Trail and the storm settles in, causing the team to stop at Outpost Camp for the night. All the time his climbing partner is asking, "What's going on?" They were guides from Canada with years of experience and knew the drill/mind/body control.

His friend, who had taken a 40' fall, was hoisted up the next day when Search and Rescue had flown up with the proper gear. The take-away from this example is, a rescue is never as expected. Rescues can turn into a crime scene. People, gear, and travel to the Portal can take hours, and night rescues for injured climbers in the upper elevations very seldom happen.

THE BEARS

"Are there really bears here?" Or how about, "Are there A LOT of bears here?" Although the California Grizzly Bear is our State Animal, and is prominently displayed on our flag, they have been extinct in California since the 1920's. Their smaller cousin, the American Black Bear, is alive and well. If you see a bear in the Whitney area, whether it is black, brown, grey, or cinnamon, it's an American Black Bear.

These questions come up all the time. We don't yet have a baseline of X number of bears per square tree to measure against, so we're not sure how many are "a lot" of bears. People always want to know about the bears, but most folks have a hard time believing what we tell them until they encounter these remarkable animals themselves. We added this chapter in the second edition, sharing some stories about our own bear experiences and observations.

Control the food source!!

We have had a few bears in the Portal; the heyday for "Boo-Boo" was about 15 animals one summer. Bears can be a complex problem. Since bears are very mobile, a terrified camper who thinks he or she will be eaten by a grizzly may report it as 800 lbs, 15' tall...and was it brown or was it black?

What was the bear doing? It went right to the ice chest and got the food! It broke into the car and got the food! It went to the food storage box and got all the food! How did it open the box? Well, it was daytime, and we didn't think bears would come out in the daytime. The best one was when a lady told Earlene, "The bear got all the food from the hidden ice chest!" Earlene asked, "where was the ice chest hidden?" ... under the table.

"Enjoyed camping & hiking & a bear entered our car & ate our food!"
- SAN JACINTO, CA

"My friend was freaked when she saw a bear"
- LOS ANGELES, CA

Like clockwork, for a few summers the bears would travel up the creek from the campground to the pond and fish along the way. When they would spot people fishing at the pond, the bear/bears would head towards the pond/people causing the people to leave in a hurry and the bears would get the stringer of fish.

Hikers are now required to carry their food in a bear resistant container overnight on the Whitney Trail. We expect these will be required state-wide before long. Even if you go where they are not required, using a bear canister is the best way to ensure you will have food to eat, and your camp won't be bothered by bears.

Each Portal campsite has a very small food box to store your supplies. You must clean it out when you check out. The problem is, people are traveling and carrying 6 days' provisions for six people. This might fill two large ice chests, plus a water container and food bag. The campsite food box will only hold about one-fourth of this, so the rest gets stored in someone's car. The car, van, or truck is broken into, the owner is cited, and all the items stored in it are covered with bear saliva, poop, and hair. The campers leave angry, and the next group arrives with their two ice chests, water container, and grocery bags of chips and muffins. The story continues until one day someone has to come and shoot the bear. We can either run out of bears or stop the cycle.

We spend many hours a year trying to show folks the cause and effect of items in their vehicle, and every year we hear the same arguments. "The van was clean! Nothing was in there except—only—just…" "I didn't have time to read the signs." "I saw the broken glass all over but thought it was kids doing the damage." "Do you REALLY have bears here?" "I'm not taking all my stuff out of the car! I'll cover it up with a blanket!" "The ice chest was empty!"

We have also watched all the "safe" methods fail—bleach, moth balls, ammonia, pepper, hot sauce, urine, taco seasoning, etc. Once a bear is rewarded by finding food, it will associate a particular sight (ice chest) or smell (white gas) and respond to it.

We now have devised a method to keep your vehicle bearproof. Bring your friend's vehicle. Leave nothing in it. Leave the windows all the way down and the trunk open.

Don't blame the bear for your behavior... (Photo by Marc Moreau)

So, what have we learned living with bears for over thirty seasons? Each bear has a personality. You can fool some of them some of the time, but by the next day they have figured you out. They can move quickly through brush or between cars unnoticed. They follow about the same paths each year, returning to areas where they found food. We know places they return to each day or each year.

They are very polite, and appear hurt if you scold them when they are taking food from cars or tables. Also, they seem to respect territory, and they like recognition. Some come by our sleeping area acting like they want to be seen, and then move on.

Bears move quietly and may appear suddenly anywhere in the area. Kathy Thompson walked out the back door one night and walked right into a bear hanging out behind the Store. Both of them were very surprised! On another evening, Doug was clearing off a table in the patio area when he realized a bear was standing behind the trees watching to see if any scraps were left from dinner.

We have watched from our trailer many times, as bears go along the rock wall past our windows. One year the pattern was to bump the corner of the trailer each time they passed. One night,

Earlene was sitting on the trailer steps when a bear walked right up to her as if no one was there. "Hey bear," she said, and the animal moved away.

One day, an experienced hiker was at the Store talking about the city folks who don't know how to protect their food. My friend told him to look out the door because a bear was tearing his pack apart as he spoke. The guy thought it was a good joke until he turned around and saw the bear and his pack heading north.

Gene and Jeannine Hauet were camp hosts at the Portal for a long time. We used to share the bear patrol in the area, moving the bears out of the parking lots and campground. There is nothing like seeing a large bear sitting in a new car or van ripping into boxes of food and drinks that people have left. We saw this happen many times—sometimes several times in one night.

Trunk storage used to be safe, but the bears figured that trick out around 1995. Now when they smell something in the trunk, they break a window, rip the back seat and rear deck apart, and pull the luggage and boxes open one by one to get at the attractant. This is not a pretty picture when the bear's work is complete. Then a Ranger will issue a citation.

Don't stay in the wilderness for a week if you are careless with food storage in your car. Here's the scenario: the day you leave, a bear breaks into the vehicle. Each additional day the bear and its buddies visit your car, removing more items. At times the roof becomes a picnic table for mass bear feedings. This problem is now being addressed by a new policy—your car will not only be ticketed, it will be towed off the mountain.

People ask us why bears don't come into the Store at night. The answer is simple: we put up the "Closed" sign!

Actually, what we do is a long and continuous process to control lack of access to food or trash. We close the kitchen one hour before the Store closes. We clean the entire Store and kitchen. We leave no trash cans outside. We clear the tables and hose the area down. The food is stored in the interior of the building, away from windows. We inspect the area about 30 minutes after we close and then again about 11:00 p.m. to make sure no one has left packs or trash on the tables. We try to keep the shower room locked

Bears can come up from the creek, down the hill, out of the bushes or down the road—in other words, from every direction.

because people could leave trash in there after we close, and bears would go in after the trash.

The camp hosts, Fish and Game staff, local sheriffs, Forest Service personnel, and the Whitney Store gang spend many hours each year making sure the bears have a safe season with no access to human food. We know from observing these bears that diligent 100% food control works. Only WE the PEOPLE can control the food cycle.

At times it may seem OK to leave things out in your camp, or "in" your car. Please understand that these slight breaches of food control can lead to a season of broken windows, lost packs, and in the final analysis, the death of a bear.

We remember one year when a bear became aggressive in search of human food. We had moved the bear into the forest several times during the season. The animal always returned, becoming habituated due to frequent and easy access to people food. After moving it into the forest once again, Doug walked back through the campground passing three campsites with food left unattended on the table. The camp host had talked to these campers. Signs are all over the area. Each table has a warning about bears, and proper food storage lockers are provided. The next morning, the bear was shot.

A young buck

Marmot going for a pot

THE WILDLIFE

Now what do you call them? Real simple—if they walk they're animals; if they fly they're birds, bats, or bees; if they bloom they're flowers—and the rest we call scrub. After spending most of our time outdoors, and in most of the Western U.S., we have observed that if you call a duck a duck, someone will help you with, "No, it's a ___." This holds true with flowers, animals, rocks, dirt, water, moss, algae, etc. We don't want to spend a lot of time on this, as there are good books on all these areas. And every few years, new books will appear with the "final interpretation." So please don't feel put out if someone asks you what something is called, and you don't know.

If you are out and about looking, smelling, feeling, listening, and even tasting, you have been touched by your experience, and the more times you expose yourself to the outs and abouts, you expand your reference database. Then you will start to see the color changes, the leaf structures, the number of needles on the pines, and the color and detail of the rock formations.

Our view is that understanding the wildlife is a lifelong process of exposure. Please don't limit yourself to what exists in written material. What you see and experience in this visit is filling your storage banks. You can be rewarded through the realization that we pass through life as a magnet, and we can attract or repel our surroundings by how we process what our experiences are. We talk with many people who just go up the Trail and down, getting to the summit as the primary objective. This is good, but if you expand your expectations into a sightseeing trip rather than simply a challenge, the encounter is very different.

Some people ask, "How do you

> "...we all saw the big ears and green eyes of a deer bedded down, looking at us like a, yes, deer in the headlights"
> - **MESSAGE BOARD**

stay in this canyon all these years?" Well, we could go on about the friends we have made over the years, the easy lifestyle, the joy of cleaning up the store every day, etc. But honestly, every day we experience something new. We know that at the beginning of the year when few campers are in the canyon, wildlife is all about. We see it during the main season as night closes in, and human activity slows down. Back it comes each year, with different snow levels, and different times of winter arrival.

The temperatures of May and June will bring a host of flowers and grasses which will bring the deer, birds, squirrels, chipmunks, mice, and more. From a different perspective, it looks like the animals have adapted to a peaceful co-existence, moving slightly away from the bustling crowds, and reappearing at quieter times.

We are including a list of birds and flowers that were experienced on several hikes by Marcyn Del Clements. (See Appendix D.) These are shared for an introduction. One can add the scrub, ground cover, and plant life that will display for limited amounts of time and frequency.

Bobcats, Po Cats and Friends

Many signs warn of bear activity, but we also see other wildlife. Deer are quite often in the area and can be a real hazard on the road driving up/down from/to town. Several springs lower down provide water and forage along the road. Near the Portal, deer can cross the road and travel up the steep banks, knocking rocks loose that tumble into the road.

Bobcats near the base of the mountain (Lone Pine Campground area) are spotted some years. Our Granddaughter, Grandson and Daughter-in-Law saw 6 bobcats on the way to school one morning. Who was going to school? Maybe everyone (people and animals). Mountain lions can sometimes be seen from just outside of town to very high on the mountain (big horn sheep and deer are a food source). We rarely have sightings of them, but often find markings and tracks in the area.

Rattlesnakes can be spotted up to 11,000' but are very rare that high. More often they are found in the lower elevations, say below 8,000' for our area; but then again, never deal in absolutes.

A general rule: Leave the snakes alone! The most common story for snake bites is, "We tried to throw rocks at it" or, "I got it with the hiking stick/branch/shovel/rake/hoe/broom and when I picked it up, I got bit!" Cutting the head off will getcha too! See, just leave them alone. If you do get struck, mosey on down to the local hospital, maybe 100 miles away. Or if you have cell coverage, Life Flight can treat you at the spot.

Racoons are a problem near town, so camp away from town or populated areas. We have seen a few in the Portal but not often; same with coyotes. Both of these guys adapt very well to human habitat, easily surviving off our carelessness. Rabid animals are always a risk, but by avoiding contact and staying aware, you should be fine. Hint: if you see an animal that looks hurt or injured and in need of help, call someone!! Don't get near or touch the animal.

Several years, we've had hikers come in who claim to have seen/heard wolves! Our first assumption was maybe they had seen coyotes. I was walking down the Trail late one night when just after Lone Pine Lake, a deer ran across the trail. This area is a great spot, level and one of the few areas with soil, so vegetation is lush. Next, I saw three wolves cross about 10' in front of me going after the deer. Note: I didn't believe these were natural wolves. All were the same size, color and had the look of the "drug plantation protection" crossbreeds that you see. This was about 10 years ago.

During the 2017 season we had at least seven sightings reported. The first few we thought, again, may have just been coyotes. But then we heard from two people who were very knowledgeable about wolves and lived in an area where they see them often. They were not concerned with the wolves being in the area, but just mentioning, "Oh by the way, we saw a wolf."

Do we have wolverines? Earlene saw a wolverine one night. Another time, I was touring with Representatives during one of the economic development projects and we drove to

> *"A family of blue grouse distracted us, and I took [dozens] of pictures of them calmly wandering along the slope, eating the crunchy willow buds"*
> - **MARCYN DEL CLEMENTS**

the Portal. On the way back to town, just as we passed the main winter gate closing, he asked, "Do you see wolverines often? I just saw one at the edge of the road."

My thoughts are, we get animals dropped off by people who once had them as a pet and then decide to return them to nature. We had a mountain lion that would walk around during the day and sleep on carpet mats outside of campers' trailers. And, a very large bear that got food out of a cabin kitchen window, walked around to the front of the cabin, and went to sleep—ignoring the people in the area. Wolves (dog/mix), tame mountain lion, tame bear and a few city snakes...and the wolverine sightings were during the same year they were spotted in other areas for the first time. Earlene doesn't believe the wolverine was anyone's pet at any time—ever!

Then there was the baby spotted skunk that walked across the floor of the store one day!

Deer mouse searching for food... beware, these critters can be carriers of the Hantavirus

WEATHER

"Well, if it isn't the floods, it's fire!"

The old story about "it rains every afternoon, so you have to be off the summit by [some magic time]" isn't here. We may have months with not a drop of rain. If we do get rain on the upper elevations, it will be hail or snow and strong winds.

Storms can move in and out quickly. Strong winds move the systems through the area, and if the wind stops the system will be static, dumping rain for hours or days. We have a closed bowl and one main stream to remove the water. To exit the canyon, you cross this stream several times, and the stream can and many times has turned into a major river. We are very lucky we are at the upper elevation. Think 10 miles down with a 4,000' change in elevation and the road can be washed out near town. Now you and your car may be in the Portal for a few days.

If that isn't a hoot, fires have caused evacuations from the area. Fires from hundreds of miles away can fill the canyon with smoke and ash making hiking/breathing very problematic, burning your eyes and irritating throat and lungs.

Storms are brought in by wind and taken out by wind. If the wind starts, with clouds moving in and building up, it could rain, turn to sleet and snow, and continue falling. If the wind stops, expect the storm to stay in the area. When the wind starts again, the storm will move.

We had about three days of pouring rain one season, where everybody was waiting to go up each day. The people coming down were giving detailed reports on how heavy the rain was, how deep it was running in the trail, where it was turning to snow, how windy it was, etc. We had a display showing every kind of foul

> "Windy, chest-high snow bluffs—
> a challenge to find the trail"
> - EARTH

weather gear on the market. The only thing keeping people dry was the bright yellow "rubber ducky" suit—something that any well-dressed, serious mountaineer would never buy or be seen wearing.

No one should go into the higher elevations during possible lightning storms. Not only to avoid lighting strikes; most people just turn around since they don't have the right gear, don't understand changing weather, and can set themselves up for exposure/hypothermia. And when the area is covered with clouds, it is impossible to see the thunderheads building or the distant lightning flashes warning the direction of the storm. Most storms will drop sleet or snow on the area above Trail Crest any time during the summer. Your summer may be three months long, but our summer is short—July plus the first three weeks of August.

Always watch for lightning. Strong winds, falling trees and branches, rock slides, and flash floods are very common in the narrow canyons. Also, during the winter runoff season, streams will swell at night due to melting action all day and travel time to get to lower elevations. If you need to do a stream crossing, plan to do it early in the morning or travel up or down canyon for a safe crossing. Never think that the stream or creek is only a foot deep, not flowing that fast, or not that cold!

Temperature extremes are common in the mountains. We had a 43-degree drop in about an hour several years ago. At higher elevations, once the sun goes down, expect the temperature to drop considerably. Above the tree line it's just plain cold every night. At Trail Camp in August, nights are in the 30's or 40's, but can easily dip to the 20's. The last thing you want to do is be tired, hungry, cold, and still have ten miles to go after dark.

We see a lot of nights in July and August when slower hikers get up to Trail Crest at 5:00 or 6:00 p.m. and insist on going to the summit. This puts them back at Trail Crest in the dark with the cold setting in. Just whip out your pocket calculator and figure the experience going down. This is obviously courting disaster and brings on what we call the "Saturday Night Special" (see page 58).

From an Expert:

Shawn Trueman, a meteorologist who is familiar with the Sierra, offers these tips for late spring to early autumn weather:

- The earlier in the day the cumulus clouds form over the mountains, the greater the likelihood of showers/thunderstorms that day. The precipitation type in these showers and thunderstorms may be rain, snow, snow or ice pellets, and/or hail.
- The clouds almost always form first over the crest and then expand east and west. However, the clouds can also form over the Great Western Divide (a range of the Sierra west of the main crest) and move eastward.
- Want to learn more? Search the Internet for upper-level wind data, and check the wind direction at 500 millibars (about 18,000 feet above sea level) at nearby stations such as Reno and Mercury, Nevada. If upper-air winds are from the south or southeast over the Sierra, there is a high probability of showers and thunderstorms. High winds from the southwest indicate that showers are not likely.
- Still curious? Search again for water-vapor satellite imagery. If you can see white over the Sierra, there is a high likelihood of showers and thunderstorms. Conversely, if the water-vapor imagery is dark (black) over the area, storms are less likely.
- From mid-autumn to mid-spring, the storm track brings low-pressure systems into California from the Pacific.

When we are asked, "What's the weather going to be?" honestly, we have no clue. From a lifetime outdoors, I know some days are better than others. So, take the gear that you need. I have worked in 20-30 degrees below to 120 above, strong winds, blowing sand/snow/ice/fog/rain and clear blue skies, and some days it seemed like the whole range of conditions. Basic assumption: "If you can't protect your body you will die." Subject someone

"Bloody Hell it's cold"
- **BALLYMENA, N. IRELAND**

"Watch for hail at the Crest!"
- **BERKELEY, CA**

to extreme heat or cold plus exposure, and add length of time into this equation. My thoughts are, plan for the worst. It is not the weather forecast that's important; it is, "Are you prepared?"

We watch NOAA.gov, the 16km infrared Western US map. That shows us the position of a system from Attu, Alaska to the Hawaiian Islands and the Western states. Why? Systems can move 40-50mph. Going out 2,000 miles west, we can see the mass of a system, high or low pressure, and the likely area the system will make landfall. That's the main search. Once the system hits land, many geologic features influence the storm as it moves east: the Coastal mountains, San Joaquin Valley, the Great Western Divide, Sequoia/Kings Canyon, and the Sierra Crest. Then in the rain shadow (our side), wind will move the system in/out. A very wet system will release much of the moisture before it can clear the ridge; expect high winds and fog/cloud cover.

Now the dealbreakers—the systems from the Gulf of Mexico. We watch the Tucson weather and if they are hit we may have a spin-off such as heavy rain/hail/lightning and "sucker hole" blue sky. These systems travel into our area and may go west into the next valley or up over our valley. Systems like this may stay several days or longer and drop 3-5 inches of water in several hours, washing out the road, turning the trails into rivers, flooding the Portal, and washing out campsites in the campground. We don't know what day or time it will happen, but it will.

On to the rain gear thing. Get that five-pound rubber suit the construction folks wear, get the pants with the bib and suspenders, the coat that hangs below your knees, and a hood. This adds about 20 pounds, but you will be dry. Or go the $500 hi-tech, just-above-the-waist jacket and after a few minutes be soaked to the core (potential for recovery). The sad fact is, there is very little product on the market that is designed for hours of heavy rain (3-5 inches an hour) with 30-50 mph wind gusts. Lean towards wool layers: socks, first layer of pants and a top layer when weather is bad; this will provide some protection. The fast wicking material will also shed your body heat. I used to think that hypothermia started around 50 degrees F (air temp). I have adjusted that to a body temp of 95 degrees F and lowering, so with wet clothing and wind without a very solid system to keep body temp in and air out, you will start to decline (potential for recovery).

OK, on a lighter note... One day we had a downpour of rain, turning the Trail into a river from hell. People were running into the store asking, "What do we do?" We knew the road was going to wash out and the store was going to be in the flood. So, we told people "get out as soon as possible—get to your car and get off the mountain." Doug Jr. began to shuttle people off the mountain, making several trips taking people into town. I suggested our staff get out quick and Myles and I would stay. Jack and Laura offered to stay and shovel, move rock and direct hikers down the National Recreation Trail. Doug Jr. called Earlene from town and said, "From town we are being hit by a very dense system." He relayed that the road was going, and flooding debris into the campgrounds." A fire crew walked up and offered to walk people down, past the flood area. People were in shock and stayed in the store, not understanding that we have three major canyons feeding the area and if the downpour continued, the road into town would be washed out. We would be dry but stranded with no road.

Myles and Jack got one of the hikers into the shower. Hypothermia had set in; several others were nearing that same stage. We were getting reports that the log bridge before Lone Pine Lake was gone and water was waist deep. The stream crossing at the North Fork was raging and about 100 hikers were stranded. Myles, Richard, and several others went up the old trail and started directing people down.

A group of about 25 started praying in the store. My thought was: get up and walk down the dry side of the canyon to the dry area of the campground, get into their cars and drive into town before the road washed out—a better prayer. God works in strange ways. They got up and went into town.

Now, the waist-deep water at the logs was not quite "waist deep." One of the stranded hikers had a phone/

"How 'bout that altitude"
- **INDIANAPOLIS, IN**

"I think I can, I think I can, give or take a little"
- **DES MOINES, IA**

Not a good time to be on the summit.

camera with video I looked at, and best I could tell, the water was just below the top of the socks of the person walking through. But how would you know how deep it may get, and how wide? Same with the North Fork crossing. On all the carry-outs, at all the logs and the North Fork crossing, the safest way is to walk into the water slowly and establish solid footing before each move through the water. Hiking poles will help.

Again, during the 2017 season the run-off was a problem for many hikers. We suggested, "just walk through the water, it is less than 9 inches, and avoid rock hopping, that may cause you to slip and fall" (potential for recovery). I think some hikers have little to no back-country experience so as the conditions change from dry to varying circumstances, they are not prepared and should consider coming back to hike when conditions are at their skill/experience level.

Check the weather, and travel out knowing projected conditions. For example, if rain is in the forecast, don't hike in the bottom of a canyon. Watch for debris flowing from down the side slopes, trees/branches blowing down, lightning, and sleet turning into snow as temperatures drop below 40 in a cold storm. Notice if there is a change in wind direction during the storm or if the wind stops and the storm has stalled. Understand storm cycles in the area: how long they last, the general pattern, and the past worst-case conditions. Storms don't just happen—"All of a sudden it's flooding!" Really?! Clear blue sky, no wind, clear for about 1,000 miles on NOAA.

YOUR SUCCESS FACTORS

<u>Physical Fitness Isn't Everything</u>
Eight Factors (other than physical fitness)
Contributing to your Ability to
Climb Mt. Whitney

- **Genetic Factors**—Size of heart, lungs, arteries, skull, brain
- **Altitude Acclimation**—Percentage of red blood cells (at what altitude do you live; have you spent some time at the Portal? It takes about 3 months to acclimate completely.)
- **Mental and Emotional Expectations**—Degree of self-confidence, tenacity, determination to reach summit
- **Level of Tolerance**—Threshold for pain, nausea, heights
- **Weather**—Temperature, precipitation, ice or snow on trail
- **Medication**—Use of pain relievers, inhalers, Diamox caps
- **Nutrition**—Carbohydrates and sugars vs. fat and proteins
- **Preparation**—Adequate clothing, equipment and supplies

The Three Big Questions

We can ask three questions and establish a fair guess about how people will do on the hike:

1. **Do you diet?**
2. **How much water/electrolytes did you drink the past several days?**
3. **Have you ever hiked over 12,000 feet?**

1. Do you diet?

If you diet, and you haven't changed your eating habits several weeks before this hike, your body may not have enough stored energy. Also, you might not bring the 4,000-6,000 calories to replace what you are using on the hike.

What we do: Eat as you hike to keep fueling your body. What we eat: Gu, Clif Bars, honey packets, candy, bread, cheese, jerky, Pop Tarts, nuts, trail mix.

2. How much water/electrolytes did you drink the past several days?

Water consumption is important days before the hike, along with electrolytes. People who train for the Badwater Race (from Death Valley to Whitney Portal in July) exercise in heat to adjust their bodies for processing large amounts of liquid.

What we do: Drink 4-6 quarts of water each day for several days prior to the hike. The day before, drink 4 quarts of electrolytes. On the day of the hike, drink 4-5 quarts of electrolytes from the Portal to Trail Camp. Purification method: Iodine (Potable Aqua) tablets – 2 per quart plus electrolyte drink. This replaces the chemicals you lose.

By eating and drinking regularly, you replace liquid and calories as you go. Doug says: "I never sweat or breathe hard. If I feel my body getting warm or flush, I slow down. Pushing your body only starts the failure cycle—rapid loss of hydration and energy, i.e. cramps, soreness, muscle fatigue, and hitting that point of exhaustion and dehydration."

How do you know what your body can do? Short, hard training will prepare your body and mind for a short, hard event. You can condition for the experience, but…look at the old, overweight construction worker who can go up and down the mountain with no problem. Wearing a pair of Broughams, bib overalls, and a cotton sweatshirt, they probably never heard of the name brand boots or gear we see on the trail. (We see all kinds of footwear—some people have even chosen to hike barefoot to the summit.)

This person has developed long term endurance by being on their feet 10-12

Marmots are quite happy at 14,000'

hours a day. His/her work includes pushing, shoving, twisting, turning, and lifting, with short bursts of high energy output followed with rest. They do this day after day, knowing that if they fail to take care of the machine and control the output, he/she will not last all day on the job.

If labor-intensive workers failed at the rate of hikers, they would not be employed, due to lack of ability to work all day every day. Their working conditions may include heat, cold, rain, snow, wind, noise, odors, etc. This makes for a total mind/body adjustment. Now if you plan to train, add to your cookbook some 10-15-mile hikes and see if you can stay alert, enjoying yourself. Try to get to the level that you can do this nonstop or at least by company rules: 15 minutes morning break, 30 minutes lunch break, and 15 minutes afternoon break.

3. Have you ever hiked over 12,000 feet?

If someone has hiked above 12,000 feet, this tells us they have not just been in California doing short coastal hikes up local mountains. They will have experienced the effect of ice-sun-wind-cold-heat-snow above tree line, and maybe learned to breathe a little differently and what to expect. Above tree line, we call it the moonscape: rocks, rocks, and more rocks. Now one must look for visual relief. Look to the macro views—far away valleys, mountains beyond, and lakes below. Enjoy the tiny streams, soaring birds, and the chance of the high-altitude flowers: sky pilot and alpine gold. Savor the glimpses of rosy finches and the pesky marmots.

Around 11,000-12,000 feet, most people who are ill prepared physically or mentally turn back. The hikers who try to carry a 50-60-pound pack to Trail Camp will see a very slow go from above Mirror Lake to Trail Camp. Doug's motto is, "One can never carry enough stuff you don't need."

"Departed at 2:30 pm - Returned 8:00—5 hr 30 min"
- **SAN DIEGO, CA**

"9.5 hours"
- **AUSTRIA**

"11 hours to top and back (73 years)"
- **MIAMI, FL**

"17 hours up and back???!!!"
- **BERKELEY, CA**

This short three-fold inquiry can give us a window into what may predict the outcome. But we also believe the most important input is if people are honest with themselves and follow sound judgement. If they are prepared mentally and physically, they will make it to the summit and back. Our experience is that those who make it are not always the extreme fitness type.

Your Mental and Physical Preparation

We remember one day we were talking about a runner from Barstow, CA, who went up and down in 3:15 hours. A customer said he had run marathons in 2:40, and it took him over 7 hours to go up and down Whitney—he didn't believe it was possible to do it in less. What he didn't understand was that running a 2:40 marathon does NOT prepare you mentally for such a climb as the Whitney Trail.

What can we learn from this? Ask yourself this question: Do you really want to make it to the summit? We're not talking about the approach that some folks take, where they will force themselves at all cost to get to the top. You need to think in terms of enjoying yourself. Think about it this way: Will I see five new flowers, five new trees, and five types of wildlife? Or will I see only the dirt and rock on the Trail two steps in front of me?

The first time up Whitney can be doomed by anxiety. People worry about "what if" this or that, "where are we?" and "how much farther?" They see people passing them and notice some piece of gear ("look, they have one of those, I should have one too"). They fall into the "should have" frame of mind: If only the weather was hotter/colder, not raining or wind not blowing.

Let's assume that you have followed a training schedule; gotten rid of excess pack weight; eaten heartily and conditioned your body to process liquid and energy; and you have gone on several long walks. The Whitney Trail to the summit is a walk, just like you would take in a mall or golf course, but less threatening. No one is likely to rob you, and you won't be caught in a crossfire of gang activity, or be struck by a flying golf club or ball.

Get to the Portal several days ahead of your hike. Take a drive to Horseshoe Meadow and walk around the area. The parking lot is 10,000+ feet elevation, and walking to the first lake gets you to around 11,000' in about six miles. This walk will let you experience the elevation, the dryness of the air, and approximates how the Whitney Trail is to the summit. Practice breathing and pace. Use pressure breathing.

We strongly urge people to use (two) walking sticks. We know they work and will make the downward walk a lot more risk free by taking the shock off your knees, ankles, and lower body. With practice, you can use the sticks to pull yourself up the trail. Now you have transferred some of the work off your legs and put your arms/upper body to work instead of just taking them along on the ride.

Let's go over some numbers that float around the climbing scene. At 14,000 feet, the air pressure is approximately 80% of that at sea level. You also lose 30% of your strength due to altitude. So, how do you recoup these losses? One good way is by reducing the weight of your pack. Carry a "go-lite" type pack—ounces, not pounds, of dead weight. Hydrate and energize your body up to the 14,000' level. Use the walking sticks and your upper body strength. Use the "pressure breath" technique—a strong exhale with a "pop" to get old air out of the lungs. If you don't clear your lungs of all the stale air, you don't have sufficient volume for fresh oxygen-carrying air that you badly need.

C.O.E. = Conservation Of Energy. Walk slowly; prevent profuse sweating and rapid breathing. Your body sweats to cool it down, and gasping for air says you're lacking oxygen. Sweat is taking liquid and chemicals from your body, and rapid breathing is also sapping vital moisture from your body.

Look at the winner of marathons. He or she is used up at the end—sometimes cramping, vomiting, or falling to the ground exhausted. Now take that same person and do the marathon in six hours, replenishing

> "After seven months of preparation of mind, gear, & body (and climbing any other mountains we could), we did it"
> - CAYCE, SC

> "...glad I bought some $4.88 water shoes at Walmart for the stream crossings"
> - MESSAGE BOARD

liquid and energy as they go, and transferring about 30% of the work to the upper body by using poles to pull themselves forward. Now when this person crosses the finish line, they should look about the same as they did when they started. Did they win? Did they see, smell, sense, or touch the world that day? Which is more important?

When we talk about slow pace, this will be different for everyone. But using the body as a guide, you will adjust to what's comfortable. A general rule we see is about 1 mile per hour up and a little faster down, for day hikers. For overnight hikers, the pack weight is the limiting factor. As people buy more security and gadgets to play with, they must stop to rest and recover from the load.

Look at the process as simple physics—a certain level of work is required to carry a given load over a particular distance. Therefore, the less load you carry, the less work is required. From a mechanical viewpoint, a car gets rid of heat through a radiator; it gets fuel from a gas tank; its surfaces that are subject to wear are cooled and lubricated by special oil; and air is forced into its combustion chamber to facilitate production of energy. Now, overload any mechanical device within the car, and watch it fail if any one of the components are lacking.

One day we got a call from a lady who was planning a group hike to Whitney. I answered a few questions, gave a few tips, and assumed they would come to hike. A few weeks after that call, the group came into the store and we talked for a while. Then I took them up the old trail just to show them where it was and give them an idea of what the Whitney Trail would be like. I noticed the lady who I had spoken to weeks before was very quiet and did not have many questions. She seemed to have a great deal of knowledge on hiking, yet allowed the others in the group to use their best judgment along the Trail as she followed along. She understood that some reassuring and encouragement could help the group accomplish their goal of reaching the summit.

A day later the group came back in with a trip report. They had successfully reached the summit and went on to tell us that the lady in the back of the group was in fact Stacy Allison, the first American woman to summit Mount Everest in September of 1988. Even though Stacy could have led the group the whole way, making all the judgment calls, she knew that monitoring their decisions and allowing the group to move at their own pace was the best way to accomplish the hike.

How Long Will It Take?

This is THE most frequently-asked question in the Store.

Why do so many people ask this question? Probably because they want to know if they are above or below average. Someone will usually dispute whatever answer is given. If the Store People tell them it takes five hours, they argue that's too fast. If the answer of 15 hours is given, they say their friend did it in 11 hours.

The reader must realize there is much more to "getting to the top" than being in good shape physically. Marathon runners have attempted the summit and failed. On the other hand, there is an amazingly steady stream of hikers who do reach the summit in one or two days without being physically fit. This is because there are a number of variables other than physical strength that contribute to each person's speed and success along their way to the top of Mt. Whitney.

Recorded in the Guest Book is a timed record for the Mountaineer's Route of 2:08:34 to the summit, and 3:23:01 round trip by Marty Hornick on September 29, 1991. This route is steeper and more direct than the Whitney Trail. A distance of 3.4 miles was wheeled in 2001. Marty's record stood for over a decade, but it was eventually toppled. Jason Lakey went up and down the Mountaineer's Route in 3:10 on August 24, 2002. And that was broken too—as of this writing, the record is 2:38 round trip, set by Matt Dubberley on August 2, 2015.

Vernon Morrison doesn't run it for speed, but one day he went up and down the Whitney Trail twice, both times in just over 3 hours. He thinks if he ran it for time, he could cut it by

"Get good boots"
- LOS ANGELES, CA

How much gear is too much gear?

20 minutes, giving a time of 2:50 or so. Someday someone will come up and do it like a marathon. An obtainable record could be somewhere around 2:30 or 2:35. It's shorter than the 26-mile marathon run.

The Whitney Trail can be done in five hours or less; most people need more time.

THE GEAR THING

I will touch briefly on gear and my personal thoughts. First, before purchasing gear that you may need, check your closet. You can probably find a substitute or something that will work. We have climbed Whitney in clothing proper for the mall or beach; and worn Vans up the North Fork, with a light dress shirt and Levi's, a 10-liter day pack, a one-quart water bottle and a few snacks. "How?" is the question. We live here with knowledge of the area and if conditions change for the gear we have, we turn around. Traveling light can increase your distance traveled. Traveling nonstop can maintain your comfort level; by stopping you may become chilled. Several options for each "need" not only adds weight, but digging for "that perfect piece" takes time and puts you at risk of forgetting to put something back in the pack.

Whitney is a four-season mountain. We have a very limited summer season when above 12,000' snow is possible 12 months a year and there are high winds over the ridges. With this background, we look at 10 months of winter gear and 2 months of spring/fall.

Below 12,000' we have late June to early September for some warm days and cool nights above freezing. So, your gear is based on your timeframe on the mountain. Before mid-June you'll need winter mountaineer gear and clothing, a four-season tent, a -0 degree sleeping bag, technical gear for snow and ice travel, and added fuel for extended length (3-4 days) to summit vs. 1-2 in the summer period. Around June 15, we'll have ten inches of snow at the Portal, with several feet of drifts at 12,000'. This does not happen every year, but it is not a rare event either. Again, we live here, and all days are great—some greater. For example, a

> "This pack weighs a ton!"
> - LONG BEACH, CA

> "Take something warm to the top! Be careful!"
> - EUGENE, OR

ten-inch overnight snowfall loads the trees, the trail, and parking lots. Cars get stuck, people are slipping and falling to get in/out of their cars, and the sun comes out—GREAT! Until the snow falls from the trees hitting hikers and tourists, the Trail turns into a river, and the stream crossings may have ice below the snow-covered rock. If this was your day, would you be ready?

My thoughts are to focus on basic functional gear that works for a broad range of conditions and temperatures. Think about the newest products on the market; they are replacing last year's greatest product. Why? Think back when the core products were wool, silk, and down. Notice how most products hint they are "Just as warm as ___" or "like___." Cotton always gets a bad rap, and rightly so. Just think how wet cotton gets at -20 degrees? Wait—it would be frozen and lock in the heat and keep wind out, well yeah... But add a silk underlayer and you are on a good foundation. Next, consider a down suit or Parka. Understand for protection you need a Parka, not a jacket—something that goes below your waist and has a wind/waistband strap inside, a tall collar and hood, sleeves with cuff bands, and double zipper for venting.

Wool socks can be 200-400-600 weight, and we recommend a wool sweater. Not the heavy material like some products, but a design that loops the wool, making an airgap to trap in your body heat and wick the moisture away.

Bring double-layer wool mittens and shell, and top off with a wool balaclava. This will function very well at extreme temperatures. Next is waterproofing shells. The colder the conditions, the less you need to worry about moisture. Wind is still a factor but at 20-below blowing ice crystals you may only need to vent your body heat out. When you have 20-above with wet snow and high winds, you need a functional shell. All shells seem to work fine for say a 15-minute downpour. You need something for 4-6 hours of high winds, 2-3-inches of snow per hour, and no cover in sight! I think the very new materials will do that (Cuban fiber system) but they are very pricey. A compromise would be a fiber material with rubber coating. "If it wicks it soaks." This translates to loss of fluids, minerals, and body heat, along with wet outer clothing. For a one-day or overnight trip and not to overspend, I think a product like Frogg Toggs or Coleman pvc/20 mil would be a very wise choice. It might not last more than a few trips but will not cost $300.00, is fairly light, and will keep you dry.

So, I will name-drop some gear/companies that have worked for me over many years. Some will sound odd, and most are not high-end trendy products. For wool, Woolpower is pricey but well-made and will last years. Choose 200-400-600 weight, 600 if it is 100 below with high winds and you're sitting on a lake ice fishing. I wear their socks, pants, suit or upper sweater, and balaclava.

For mountaineering boots, I use Zamberlan. Maybe they're a few ounces heavier than other brands but they will last years, and out of the box you will know the difference—a first quality product. Several other good German or Italian products are available to check out. Note the difference between "lightweight hiking boots," "mountaineering boots," and "full winter mountaineering boots."

For a coat, Cabela makes a nice down jacket called "Extreme Hunter Parka." It is heavy material but good for 30 degrees below. I'm not sure you would ever need a four-season coat unless you plan a multi-day trip in severe weather. Consider things not working out according to plan, such as heavy snow making it impossible to travel for several days.

Doug Jr. and I have the "old big blue suits." We could never use the pants, they are just way too hot. The coats worked very well in subzero conditions. We wore these coats many days in Utah as we worked under an umbrella, measuring angles and distances. (The umbrella was used to keep the sun off the instruments, so the readings were not influenced.) This coat is still my go-to if I need extreme cold weather gear. It cost about $150.00 thirty or forty years ago.

Regarding tents, Doug Jr. says, "You walk all night." So he knows I will never carry a tent. I did a test on a bivy for a name company. It was a great design—roomy, with walls about 8" high, and it had a mesh top for ventilation. The rain fly system was put to the test in a snowstorm, with fog and freezing conditions during the night. Ice formed on the fly from the fog, and the sleeping bag became a shell of ice. The early-morning fog brought the moisture dripping down from the fly onto the bag and onto the floor of the bivy, soaking all the gear.

I do own a four-season tent that can withstand very high wind, sleeps 3 with gear, and is tall enough that you can stand up and move around in it. Why? OK, so Doug Jr. and I were on a winter trip and decided to test out a new concept of a tin foil liner, a $29.95 White Front/ Walmart/Whatever tent. As we reached the ridge a storm blasted us with whiteout conditions, and 30-40 mph wind gusts with heavy snowfall. We lost visibility instantly. Our only option was to get cover from the storm. I got Doug Jr. and our packs into the tent as I tried to secure it down the best I could with stakes. Doug Jr. held the front end down as I climbed in. For the remainder of that day and night, we kicked snow off the top and sides from inside to keep the tent from collapsing on us. Sometime the next day we were able to get out and start down. The tin foil worked perfectly. Our body condensation stuck to the foil and froze instantly. We had a closed shell, airtight except for the front door system, that had "way too short" ties and a zipper. Other than that, the tent fulfilled the test.

Our experience that day and night is the reason we will never be cramped in a tent again, sleeping on wet ground and covered in snow and ice, with no room to cook or even turn over. The only reason we did OK that night was that we had enough layers, very warm bags, and we stopped immediately to get out of the elements and maintain our body temperature. If we hadn't done these things, well you know in the climbing world the saying is, "Day of the service, color of the suit, and order flowers." This is why you should not rely on the weather forecast, but instead prepare for the worst every trip.

Bottom line: bring a four-season, two-person tent or bivy. Maybe one is not enough—or sleep out with a tarp. This brings us to sleeping bags, and how/where to set up your sleeping area. Just get a very warm bag. If the manufacturer says warm to 30 degrees, get the bag warm to 10 degrees. Down is lighter than synthetic but if it gets wet you'll have problems. Check for foot box design and waist room, either the mummy or conventional design. Use a ground pad or air mattress, full length or 3/4 coverage. A ground cover is not a bad idea as a vapor barrier from the ground moisture. Hint: check for a level spot above a natural slope for runoff. If the area is barren—there's not a twig or a blade of grass—you might be in a flood zone or avalanche chute. Look around; does this seem like a safe area? Camp away from water or meadows, off of ridges and high elevation. Look for downed trees, dead trees standing, and the growth pattern of the trees. What direction are the prevailing winds blowing? Check for animal use trails; you may notice low ground cover or plants eaten by animals if the tips are gone as if they were snipped or cut. Food sources for bears are good to check during the season. If the berries are ripe, will I camp near or under a food source?

Packs

By using a pack, remember you are adding the dead weight of the pack to your load. The top considerations are comfort, proper fit, and the loading system. Packs are like cars; one company put in a cup holder, so the next will put in ten. Another company's pack has 47 pockets plus a tube hole compartment for your charger/headphones. A good pack will have one main compartment, and a comfortable waist support and shoulder strap system with enough straps to secure the load and balance the pack. "Well, no, it isn't waterproof, but we will sell you a cover for the pack."

The one-day Whitney trip can be done using a very small day pack, say a 30-liter or 40-liter at the most. If you plan to stay one night, sleep at Outpost Camp so you can cut your gear weight/volume down to about 30-40 liters for the upper 7 miles of the Trail (vs. upper 4.5 miles). There are many new companies out now that have cut pack weight down, but if you only plan to do a few hikes a year, and mostly day hikes, think about renting a pack/tent/bag. With the money you save you could buy a good pair of boots and an ultra-light day pack.

I always hear about the "10 Essentials List." Well, the first thing that pops into my head is sales and gimmicks. Why not 25 or 30? The list could be endless. I reference it to what on the 10 list could be eliminated with a plan, experience, and a turnaround point. Several things are very basic and you should already have them: a flashlight, batteries, matches/lighter, a simple first aid kit, a map of the area, bleach for water purification (2 drops per quart), aspirin/Ibuprofen, a large trash bag, a small roll of duct tape, a very small knife, and one thing I would add is a signal mirror (and practice how to use it). Secure all of the essentials in a separate pouch…Oh, and some mountain money (TP) with your WAG Bag.

Luxury items

Luxury items or "security blankets."

These are things that serve little to no purpose, but you take if you always carry them and never use them. When Khrushchev asked Nixon, "What is an electrical lemon squeezer?" Nixon replied, "All middle-class Americans have one." That kind of stuff.

Non-luxury items

Do take an extra pair of socks, plastic utensils, a few paper towels, and a very small bowl/plate for an overnight trip. If you plan to cook or eat out of the bag, you will need to wash your kitchen items. So, bring a small amount of soap—recall the bleach? Two drops in your rinse water will kill the bugs, then air dry.

Food

Take what you would normally eat. Packaged foods are very high in sodium and will take time to prepare. A trick is to find dehydrated products at your local grocery store, count your meals, and share sealed items if you are going with a group. Now the touchy subject. Don't take food/water from anyone else. If you're considering it, always check the date on packaged store-bought items, sealed or unopened food. But never take food they made last month or got from a through-hiker or from a hiker box. They might mean well but this could be risky, and if you have a sensitive system you should protect yourself. Stick with your own food; you know if it is fresh and not likely to be contaminated. Same with water, drink only from your source.

The food you take can make all the difference in your hike.

Don't bring any food items that you haven't eaten before. Figure out how to cook/mix it, and if you can stand to look at it! Does it pass the 45-minute test before you run into the woods, WAG Bag in hand? Think about your digestive system when mixing many of the electrolyte/energy supplement, quick recovery, performance GU's, gels, and drink additives. Are you making yourself sick with the cocktail of chemicals contained in these products? We recommend using natural products like honey for a sugar fix, bananas for potassium, oranges, apples, avocado, peanut butter, whole grain items (real, not the colored brown white bread), cheese, chocolate, raisins, dried cranberries, fruit wraps, nuts, and some dried meat. How about taking some salty items such as crackers/chips? Test all this on your practice hikes. See how it packs and if it stays fresh during the day. My long-time climbing partner made a grain loaf that had about all of the above in it plus rice and seeds. We could eat for days on one loaf.

How do you carry that bear can? A simple method: place low in your pack and fill it with items you won't use as you hike such as extra clothing, stove, gas, etc. You only need to put food/scented items in the can when you stop and leave these items out unprotected. If you have them protected on your person you are fine. Note: never place food or scented items in your tent. (Oh, ya, don't use your food sack as a pillow.) That handy bear can will also serve as a seat or back rest. NEVER put your used WAG Bag in the canister (unless you want to, personal choice I guess).

MOONLIGHT HIKING

Let's talk about the moonlight hike—when to leave, what to expect, and how many days before and after the full moon you can do it. Climbing the mountain at night has the potential for a unique and very beautiful wilderness experience. There is greater solitude, and moonlight shining on the granite walls is truly awesome.

Plan to arrive at the Portal early in the day so you can spend the afternoon resting and adjusting to the area. A few days in the family campground would be ideal, making the full moon trip part of a vacation. Also, this gives you time to gather information about weather and trail conditions from hikers coming down off the mountain.

Timing: Expect to leave the Portal area around 12:00-12:30 a.m. If you leave before midnight, you need an overnight permit. Go slow and steady. It will be cool, and the higher up you go, the colder it will get. As you get sleepier, you will slow down, so watch your time between key landmarks. Outpost Camp is 1/3 of the way; Trail Camp is halfway; and Trail Crest is 2/3. The trick is to keep moving, reaching Trail Crest at sunup. That is an experience in itself. Complete the last section as the sun rises in the east. This should put you at the summit around 7:00-8:00 a.m. Most mornings, this will allow you to be the first to sign the register.

When to Go: You can see well enough about three days before and after the full moon. This gives you a window of about seven days per month. July and August are the best choices. You can try this in June if all the snow is off the trail, but most years it is still too cold to do the hike at night. Any melt water will freeze and make the trip a safety call. A thin layer of "black ice" forms over the rocks. It is very hard to see, or distinguish from running water. In a dry year, if the weather holds, you can do it in September.

When to Stop: If a wind/storm comes up, do not continue. Head back down. If the wind is blowing at lower elevations, expect what we call the "hawk" at upper elevations. This is wind that zaps all your body heat and is so strong that forward motion stops, and balance is hard to maintain. Remember, for all practical purposes, Trail Crest is the summit—you can see into the back country, you are at 13,645 elevation, and you are within a stone's throw of the hut—well, almost.

"Do it at night"
- BREMERTON, WA

"Bright moonlight!!!"
- HACIENDA HEIGHTS, CA

ZONE 4

ZONE 3

ZONE 2

ZONE 1

THE FOUR ZONES

Be aware of your location, time of day, elevation, distance to trailhead and to a safe zone. Also, who, what, why, where and when. These are the important questions you'll need to answer if there is trouble.

1. **Who are you in a group?** (leader/follower, experienced/newbie)
2. **What are the conditions?** What happened?
3. **Why did it happen?** Why did they fall crossing a creek? Did they fall off the trail?
4. **Where?** Location and relationship to help?
5. **When?** Hours ago? Did your group fail to plan/follow your plan?
6. This is the trigger event when you need to consider all of the above and now, **what steps you need to take to get to a safe zone.**

We process a response constantly for our environment, at home, work, school, store, travel, changing locations. When we encounter a new/different environment we draw from our past experience and adapt to protect ourselves. But if we are not aware of the new environment, we may formulate a risky set of assumptions and compound the situation by not adjusting as conditions indicate a modification is needed.

Simple example: You understand the mountains are "cold" (what is cold!?) You dress very warm: underlayer, second layer, and a jacket to start the hike. In a very short time you will become overheated. How do you react? You will need to remove

> "Water is readily available up to Trail Camp in lakes and streams. After the snow melts off, there is no surface water available above 12,400 ft. Plan on taking 3 liters to the summit from Trail Camp."
> - US FOREST SERVICE

clothing.... Are you comfortable undressing on the trail? The other argument is starting the Trail wearing shorts and a light shirt. But now a weather system has moved in overnight and the trailhead temperature is 27 degrees. Either condition requires adaptation. How do you react to change? What about changes in a group situation—Do you follow or lead?

This brings us into the pre-trip planning, and building a strong basic framework by expanding your experiences and exposure to the conditions you "may" encounter. How do you react when confronted with a rapidly changing environment? (The big picture is physical, emotional and physiological response).

We see many hikers on their first-ever long hike. Never have they been above 5,000' elevation, and they may or may not have researched the area. Or they are relying on the "group leader." (He/she has the permit and extra space, so I will go). History shows that most will make the trip, maybe develop a few blisters, go home tired and sore, and swear they will never do it again. This is normal for good weather, stable trail conditions, no snow/ice on the trail, water available on the switchbacks (22-25), and no one in the group needing much help. Group support is very critical! A few words of encouragement along the way will always help.

Now the trail:

Zone 1: The first four miles offer very easy travel on a wide, gentle, tree-covered trail with water available, and the temperatures are normally mild during June–September.

Zone 2: Miles four - six, conditions change rapidly as you enter 11,000-12,000'. The Trail is very rocky/slick and there is no coverage from the sun exposure.

Zone 3: Miles six–nine, the Trail is somewhat better, but you can encounter sections of ice and loose rock on the trail. At elevation 12,000-13,500,' concern can arise regarding the loss of energy and time spent on the Trail to reach this area. This is a great section for a day hike and a good turnaround point.

Zone 4: Miles nine-eleven, the Trail is very rough, rocky with slick slabs, and uneven in sections. At elevation 13,500-14,500, high wind gusts are possible. There is full sun exposure, no water source, and travel will be slower.

Zone four is the critical zone for many reasons—some real, some imagined. There is exposure to the elevation, dehydration, exhaustion from the hike to this zone, cold due to inadequate clothing (No gloves/hat/long pants/dry socks), and the chance for a weather system to move through. Rain is unlikely at this elevation, but sleet/hail, lightning or snow and strong wind gusts are common. It is critical to watch for incoming systems, and the direction the systems are moving (we get very localized systems). If a party member slips and twists an ankle or shows any sign of AMS/hypothermia, getting out of this zone ASAP is the wisest choice. Get to a lower elevation to find protection from the wind/cold and to lessen the side effects of the elevation.

As you go down, Zone four to three is the transitional zone. Things will begin to improve but it is still a high probability area for snow/strong winds and ice on the trail. There is no landing area in this zone for air search and rescue, and six to nine miles for a ground rescue takes at least six to nine hours. From 12,000' to 10,000', snow can drift and cover the trail. This area is very rugged terrain with steep drop-offs, making cross-country travel dangerous. From zones four to three, when snow starts to build and the system has stalled (no wind), one should travel to a lower elevation without delay. Waiting a storm out at 12,000' may turn into enduring very strong winds, very cold temperatures, and the Trail below may get covered by snow with three to four-foot drifts.

Zone three to two includes Trail Camp where there is water, people, and a landing area if a helicopter is available (many times one is not available). You may find medical help—EMT/First responder/firemen/police/nurses/doctors in this zone. This is a good area to get very current trail conditions as many have hiked up shortly before you. Trail Camp area is

> "One path became several paths and then became no path. We ended up getting lost. What should have been a simple descent turned into a bit of a problem"
> - **MESSAGE BOARD**

View of Consultation Lake, Trail Camp, Mt. Muir & Mt. Whitney from Mt Irvine: Zones 3 & 4.

a possible safe zone with the chance of food, shelter, extra clothing and first aid material. Depending on the season, any travel above 12,000' will be limited; if a strong system moves into zone four, zone three travel will need to focus on reaching 10,000' level, say Outpost Camp area where there is water, tree coverage, and a bit more protection from wind and temperatures. This zone will be cold but not as cold as zone four. This area of the Trail will collect snow but with the tree coverage/protection from sun exposure and hash marking on the trees, reaching the Portal is most probable.

From Zone two to one, there is increasingly easier travel. The Portal is in sight, there is some cell coverage, and once word arrives in the Portal, it's a four- to six-hour walk-up if needed for a rescue.

Notice the suggestion "you" need to travel down: Summit to Trail Crest to Trail Camp to Outpost to Portal. Limiting the time in each zone will increase your ability to remove yourself from the elements that may lead to problems: cold, elevation, lack of water, weather conditions, and gear shortage will be less problematic the lower you are.

THINGS TO REMEMBER

The threes of survival:
    3 **Minutes** no air
    3 **Hours** no heat
    3 **Days** no water
    3 **Weeks** no food

S   STOP
T   THINK
O   OBSERVE
P   PLAN

Fumble > Hypothermia
Stumble
Tumble > Motor function
Mumble
Grumble > Mental - Intellectual

Now some tips for a fall into icy water:
    60 seconds to adjust to the sudden shock
    10 minutes to get out
    60 minutes to get your core temperature back to 95 degrees

Leave No Trace — 7 elements:

1. Plan ahead and prepare
2. Travel and camp on durable surfaces
3. Dispose of waste properly
4. Leave what you find
5. Minimize campfire impacts
6. Respect wildlife
7. Be considerate of other visitors
    *(Visit **lnt.org** for more information)*

Depending on the rescue circumstances, you may end up in Fresno.

IMPORTANT
CELL PHONES

911 may work, depending on your location. A trick on your cell phone is: If you can see the valley, you may have coverage. Stand facing the valley/town, turn your phone off and turn it back on. This causes your phone to search for coverage as it powers up. Digital signal is about 10 miles. At the summit, we are about 14 miles from the towers. The towers are aligned north to south for coverage on Highway 395. AT&T and Verizon are the main providers for the area. Those systems that say "No roaming fee" … Hint: No service is why no fee. Some international phones work but most require an additional service plan.

You will get a quicker response by dialing Inyo County Search & Rescue/Sheriff's dispatch at
760-878-0383
Carry this number with you; it can help expedite the rescue process and may even save a life.

UNPLANNED ACTS

Accidents are the worst kind of unplanned acts that we see all too often.

When did the accident start? There is a long list of steps that lead to the final act. These include training, building experience from a variety of conditioning hikes, and understanding your medical history. In other words, an understanding and awareness of any restrictions and were/are they followed? So, what can you do to try to avoid an accident?

Plan for the climb. At least one day before the hike, plan to arrive at the area to help adjust to the changing environment. Hydrate with electrolytes and manage diet to maintain chemical balance. Increase food intake for energy.

Time. Select start time/permit date (May/early-June to mid-October/early-November or "dying season"—see page 127).

Did assumption of use of gear offset the need to establish a comfort level with gear? Just purchasing the gear may in fact be a strong indication of false security. An individual traveling into terrain that requires advanced training may fail to contemplate surface conditions during the day. A surface of snow can turn to sheet ice caused by sun softening the surface, onset by cloud coverage, with light wind current and sun exposure changing during the day. Just the temperature change from day to night can create very dangerous conditions.

Traveling from Trail Camp onto the snow slope during mid-morning can be easily navigated with limited snow travel experience. Six hours later

> "...many backpackers expect their trips to be peril-free strolls through the woods. If so, they should do their best to achieve that end, by hiking always in sizeable groups on easy, well-marked trails, in temperate weather, rather than courting 'adventure,' and then demanding to be bailed out when Adventure shows its darker side"
> - J. ROBLEE

on the down climb the surface is rock hard ice; what do you do? Without experience, traveling onto the slope may be fatal. Taking an avalanche course may introduce you to the advanced skills. We very seldom have avalanches; it's mainly rockfall that creates the slide. Most often these occur out of the traveled area, so understanding the terrain becomes a major factor each season.

Zone four will require a different response during the transitions from winter to spring, summer to fall. We have many days late June to mid-September with very little weather change, sunny days, with light to no wind. Overnight temperatures are above freezing, and most seasons we only see about three to five days of light rain in a few hours of the late afternoon or evening. This tends to result in complacency, and when a major storm moves in people are not prepared. Adding to the equation is the permit pressure: "This is the once-in-a-lifetime day and I have to go!"

Will you take a solo hike or go with a group? Each will have very different dynamics. A solo hiker may be very experienced, and most will never read this book. They have acquired the skills needed and have hiked many miles over varying conditions. The most likely problem factor is failure to stay focused, since the Trail is very mundane.

Group travel is another entire topic of its own. Variables include size of the group, leader/co-leader, followers, support from dynamics, or pressure to go/return, pace, rest stops, clothing stops, gear adjustments, and prior experience with the group. Is this a family hike, meet-up, or active hiking group? Or is this just another weekly/monthly hike? Can you rely on support if needed? Will they leave you?

What are the group dynamics when conditions change? Experience level is a factor. What happens when conditions indicate the need for SKA's (Skills, Knowledge, and Abilities) is beyond one or several members of the group? When a minor or major mishap occurs, can the group assess the severity of the event and react competently? What about while on the mountain? Can the group return safely to the Portal?

We see many different reactions once any open wound is encountered, or a person is unconscious or unresponsive (aka "dead"). If in a very rare occurrence someone deceases on the mountain, can the group return safely to the Portal?

This event may be experienced during a snowstorm, lightning strike or rockfall caused by a slide. This puts the entire group at risk. How is the scenario approached? A group member is lagging behind? The (inexperienced) "leader" just got the permit! What is a leader? Is this a march or a hike?

T.O.T. = Tag on toe. I once called a rescue for a person that was down on the trail; we heard the helicopter flying around for quite some time. I thought with the details I had reported they would fly to the location, pick the person up, and fly on to the hospital. That night Doug Jr. was in town talking to his buddies from Search and Rescue. They said, "We thought your Dad was losing it! We didn't see the group of six helping anyone, we couldn't find a person needing help!" One of the crew spotted a blue tarp so they landed and under the tarp was a body—tag on toe "body." We later asked about details of the six helpers. Consensus was, this person's hike was over and they could do no more for the person, so the vote was to continue to the summit.

We have always respected the privacy of accident details. I have heard many comments about how a detailed recap of each accident may avoid another accident. While that is an honorable assumption, climbing history has enough information to discredit it. I have added throughout the book (noted in parentheses) conditions that potentially may lead to a fatality/body recovery. I will give a brief overview of these conditions.

Slips and Falls

What are some reasons for slips and falls? This can lead to very serious problems. There are many causes including lack of focus, improper gear, failure to change foot placement, distance between steps, not maintaining balance before moving forward/ up and down, not testing each step as

"Try acclimatizing"
- SEATTLE, WA

Report Emergencies to Inyo County Sheriff's Department
760-878-0383   OR   911

EMERGENCY REPORTING INSTRUCTIONS

1. Ensure your own safety!
2. Verify that the victim wants help.
3. Gather information and assess the situation.
4. Attempt self-rescue, if it is safe and feasible.
5. Contact the Inyo County Sheriff, at 911, or 760-878-0383.
6. Follow instructions given by Sheriff.
7. Remain available for questions.

If victim self-rescues, moves or leaves the area, contact the Sheriff immediately!

Reporting Party Information: (Name and contact information)

Victim Information: (Name, age, physical description contact information)

Nature of Problem:

Last Known Location of Victim:

Brief History of Events leading up to emergency:

Report Emergencies to Inyo County Sheriff's Department
760-878-0383   OR   911

Report Emergencies to Inyo County Sheriff's Department
760-878-0383   OR   911

Additional Information:
Include any information that would help rescuers locate, treat and evacuate the victim. Include information such as your plan of action, who is with the victim, signs and symptoms of illness or injury, relevant medical history etc.

Inyo County Preventative Search & Rescue

The primary purpose of "PSAR" is to help wilderness users avoid needing to be rescued by providing education about the potential hazards involved in the wilderness setting, as well as the time, equipment and physical conditioning required to complete a planned outing or hike safely.

- Give your trip itinerary to a responsible party.
- Agree on a procedure for contacting the authorities if you do not report in to your responsible party by a certain time.
- Check road conditions, trail conditions and weather conditions and check frequently prior to and during your wilderness travel.
- You are most likely to suffer from: Acute Mountain Sickness (AMS), dehydration and inadequate physical preparation if you are traveling a long distance and to high altitude.
- Plan an extra day to acclimate at 8,500-10,000 ft with easy hikes and hydration. Pre-trip physical conditioning is beneficial.
- The weather can change very quickly. Know when to make the decision to turn back and return safely to the trailhead.
- Establish a cut-off time to turnaround based actual progress.
- Do not allow sick, injured or physically compromised hikers to separate from your group and ascend or descend by themselves. Doing so is a significant cause of rescues and recoveries.
- Ensure that your group members have the "Essentials" needed for safe travel. (Extra clothing, food, water/filter, emergency shelter, illumination, navigation knowledge, sun protection and first-aid)
- Larger groups can benefit from having hand-held radios.

Have a safe trip.   Inyo County Sheriff's Search & Rescue   00418
DONATE: www.Inyosar.com   PO Box 982, Bishop, CA 93515
Report Emergencies to Inyo County Sheriff's Department
760-878-0383   OR   911

conditions change. Take the time to place, test, load, then move, using your boots to the maximum advantage (soft sided boots may not offer enough support on uneven terrain). Also, the composite of sole material may change as temperatures change, the lug pattern of a sole may not make contact on uneven surface or may jamb with too much friction causing you to lose balance (very critical when descending). The tread may become filled with snow, and thus lose traction. The Trail surface can change from smooth slab to broken rock and uneven steps (16-18 inches), causing excessive downward pressure to maintain balance.

We'll list a few examples: Traveling off trail a few feet to take a short break, it is likely to be a surface with loose rock, and one foot on a rock that moves is enough to cause a loss of balance. This may lead to the "jump" to regain balance which compounds the fall by the other foot landing on a loose rock. You could lodge your foot in between two rocks, locking that foot in place as your forward body motion results in severe damage to that foot/ankle/knee/hip, or causes you to fall—which can lead to upper body/head injuries. Envision a steep trail section. You step off, get one foot lodged between two rocks as you fall forward, and now you do not just fall your height, but add in the slope angle and distance of the slope and your body mass as additional force. You may have heard climbers talk about "How to Fall?" "Tuck and roll, keep falling, and look where to land." Climbers know the risk of falling with every move. How do you avoid falling?

Now add slick surfaces, wet moss, slime/rot on wood, ice, snow, snow over ice, thin layer of ice over the surface, plus wind and lightning conditions. In a solid wind event, you can adjust to conditions, but wind gusts can be very dangerous. Have you ever encountered these conditions before?

Say a person is new to hiking, lives in an urban area, is not exposed to rapidly changing conditions, and is now exhausted. This person is facing cold and dark, weather, they were left by their hiking party, and they are now distracted/confused by losing the Trail and compounding the situation by several incorrect decisions: a) I will find the trail lower down; b) I think this is the correct canyon, I just need to climb down this short face/cliff; c) I see lights over there; d) I will just wait for help.

Stream crossings on the Whitney Trail may require walking in the water to avoid a fall. Walking in the water on slick rocks will require a steady foot placement. Slow, methodical travel will get you across safely. Jumping rock to rock is an option for some, but at what risk?

Let's now focus on the individual. How many hours of sleep did they get before the hike? What is their general physical condition, age, experience, willingness to follow suggestions, map reading ability, eyesight, need for glasses or contact lenses, tolerance for discomfort, and quite simply put, "a quitter or fighter"? How adaptable are they to rapidly changing conditions and expected outcomes? If "this-then" analysis comes into play, the group dynamics is a very critical element. What, if anything, will the group do to help?

Many slips and falls are on the descent of a climb—not just on Whitney—so this becomes the focus of many accidents. Why on the way down? And, if left by others in the group, the stranded person is at the mercy of his/her ability. Let's use a model to compare possible outcomes.

An unconditioned, middle-aged male (40s to 60s) drove to the Portal, slept 3 hours, and joined a meet-up group at 2:00 a.m. The leader says, "I know the trail, I was up here once but didn't summit. I will make it this time even if it kills me." Several others in the group have limited experience but are very strong; they work out three times a week for 45 minutes. We will call the future recovery Clyde. The group starts up the Trail at a rapid rate, one and a half miles an hour. They take short breaks, and no one is watching the trail/water/food consumption of the eight people.

Three are doing well, two are lagging behind, one we think just dropped out and returned to the Portal and by mile four, two are way ahead, out of sight. At mile six,

> "...after Outpost Camp, we went left and unknowingly lost the trail and climbed a steep hill next to a waterfall"
> **- MESSAGE BOARD**

12,000', the cold has now become a problem for several wearing shorts and no gloves or head protection, but the sun is rising. The group is now minus the two ahead and the one that turned back (make note of this). The remaining five now start the switchbacks. Quickly, two fall behind; the other three move ahead, passing each other off and on. As other hikers come down the Trail they report light wind and it is very cold, so they only spent enough time to sign in and quickly left the summit.

The three reach Trail Crest after six and a half hours on the trail. After about fifteen minutes, the "leader" and other person reach Trail Crest. One of the three now has a severe headache, is vomiting, and says after a short break he "will join the group heading up." He admits he didn't drink or eat enough, and now his urine is dark yellow and he is cramping. It is very cold now at 13,000' but there are only a couple miles left to reach the summit.

Look at the picture now: out of the eight, two are MIA (went ahead), one definitely MIA (returned to Portal), one is puking and pooping at Trail Crest, and the remaining four head towards the summit. They struggle to maintain a one to one and one-half mile an hour pace and near the summit in nine hours. As they ascend the last section, the two that left the group before Trail Camp are now heading down. They confirm it is cold and they wanted to wait but didn't have jackets or gloves, and they are out of water. They say they "will check on the guy that was not doing well." (These two reached the summit at 12:17. Not bad; they signed in and started down.)

On the slab area just past Keeler Needle, one slips and twists his ankle. His wrist is cut from hitting a rock and his glasses are broken. He tells the other hiker that he is fine, go ahead and he will catch up. Time now is 2:00 p.m., the wind has picked up, and more hikers are heading to the summit. Clyde moves off the Trail to rest and check his ankle/wrist and tape his glasses. He is thinking, "I bet the hiking poles would have helped getting down! Oh well. It's all downhill and I will walk slow and rest often." He reaches Trail Crest around 4:30 and finds no sign of anyone in the group. He talks with other hikers but doesn't seem concerned with getting down.

His wrist is now throbbing, and he is out of water. The sun is now on the west side and the temperature is 43 degrees. He is thinking long pants would be nice, a hat and gloves too. Clyde starts down the switchbacks. His balance is off, and he slips several more times. The sun is down now with few hikers going up and many coming down. He still maintains he is moving slow but will be okay. Clyde walks into Trail Camp at dark, finds water, and rests for a few minutes. He searches for his headlamp but finds that the plastic cover broke on one of his falls. By luck, holding it a certain way it works. Clyde loses the Trail out of Trail Camp. He searches for a few minutes and sees lights in the distance. He heads over and down towards the trail. Clyde isn't found for two days. By then it is too late.

The first member of the party did return to the Portal but didn't have keys to the car, so he waited all day, pacing the Portal. One of the two that summitted early and said they would check on the person at Trail Crest discovered he wasn't there (later that night he walked into Trail Camp and spent a cold, uncomfortable night, then walked down the next morning). The remaining four reached the Portal at 11:10 p.m. about 1/2 mile apart, all assuming Clyde was on his way down and had joined with the person that was sick at Trail Crest. The group starts to leave since Clyde drove his own vehicle and no one had said anyone was hurt, just that a guy was moving slow and last seen around Trail Camp.

You now have the typical slip-and-fall accident. The person is alone, separated from his group, darkness is a factor, fatigue is a factor, and a minor injury slowing the person down is a factor. Also, he doesn't know the area and the locations of drop offs if the Trail is not followed, and his physical and mental state is compromised after extended hours of exertion.

It's a similar story for the typical North Fork accident. The assumed leaders are not familiar with the route or it becomes a "team effort" to

> "Most people we met on the trail did not have a map nor did they have a working understanding of where the trail went"
> - **MESSAGE BOARD**

explore a new route to the summit. Errors lower on the mountain cause long delays in reaching the upper elevation. Then hikers are benighted and/or continue travel in the darkness and fall (potential for recovery).

During one period while building the new Store, Doug Jr. and I lived in his camper that was parked behind the building. We would get up around 5:00 a.m. and work till 7-8:00 p.m. We lived off canned food and crackers, and about every third day we would go into town for a shower and a hot meal. Each day got colder, and more storms came as the season was changing. The Whitney ranger would stop by about once a week to chat. She later told us it was just to check and see if we were still alive! On her last check-in, I was on the floor in the dark doing tile work, Doug Jr. had just left, and I had the truck parked facing downhill so when the snow reached the bottom of the truck, I would drive down.

One night during this period I drove somewhere. Doug Jr. later asked if I had noticed a guy walking down the road—he'd walked by the Store. I hadn't seen him. It was snowing and very cold. Doug Jr. thought we should look for him, so we drove around the area but could not find him. Several days later we came into the Store and found him lying wrapped around the heater we had for drying out the joint compound on the drywall.

He had lost his gloves at the notch on the Mountaineer's Route, spent at least one night at 14,000' and somehow got down. His hands, face and feet were severely frostbitten. One of the guys I had surveyed with was with us and took the guy to the hospital. Several additional experiences with more of these exposure events led us to believe that not only is there physical damage done but, in these cases, it can lead to emotional baggage later.

> "We had 'hiked' Mt. Kilamanjaro and other long treks...but this was very different."
> - **MESSAGE BOARD**

NOW THE PHYSIOLOGY: THE HIPPOS—OR IS IT THE HYPOS?

Let's take a look at what the body may have a reaction to before, during, and after the hike.

Assume first you have a very detailed physical exam including a blood profile, stress test, EKG, VO2max analysis, and a review of your medical history. This is a baseline from which you can start your training program and monitor any changes. Does this take three months? Six months? Or a longer program, or nothing at all? What is the goal? Lift 375 pounds? Run a 100 meter or a 5K? One season we reported five fatalities from heart related problems. All were in their mid-60's, four males and one female. Were there pre-existing conditions? Was elevation a factor? All events took place between 10,000' and 12,000', with no weather issues, during mid-season. Were they all from "natural causes"? Would a prior medical exam have detected any probable risk? From years of talking with many hikers, the training regimen ranged from, "I just got out of the truck and took off," to "I have trained at least a year for the hike." I hear of many saying they did the Five Peaks or Cactus-to-Clouds, Rim-to-Rim, Wonder Trail, or Half Dome. Most likely, a person with an active job on their feet for long periods of time will do the trip with less training. A three-day-a-week gym program, 45 minutes a session, not so much.

Now you have a background on your health, physical condition, and possible risk factors. Oh, and tell your doctor about your plans for a hike from sea level to 14,508' in a day or two carrying a 50-plus-pound pack. And possibly sleeping at 12,000' with no prior exposure to elevation over

> "...we still had a long way to go to reach Whitney Portal. Hiking out, it turned out, was actually the most difficult part of the day"
> - BENJAMIN SPILLMAN, OUTDOORS WRITER, RENO GAZETTE

8,500' (when you did Half Dome), which is the elevation of the Portal—where you begin your Whitney hike.

When do things start to happen with your body? First there is the adjustment to the air quality and dryness of the desert, and possible allergic reactions to a new environment. Then the adjustment to extreme heat in the valley with temperatures reaching 105 degrees, and then 20 miles away the daytime temps are in the low 40's and mid 30's at night on the mountain. At 12,000' the environment changes again in a short time duration. Consider the time zone changes/jet lag if flying cross-country. Or, traffic conditions. Are you from a large population center? You escape the gridlock several hours before reaching our area, but did the drive add more stress? Choosing your airport route to the area can be critical! For example, your flight lands at LAX in Los Angeles at 4:37 p.m. on Friday. It is 200 miles from Lone Pine. You find the rental car company. They may have a car for you, so you go to the lot, which adds two hours and change. Let's say you leave in the rental car at 7:00 p.m. and get on the 405 freeway heading north. The first few turns you take are wrong, so you end up backtracking to get going in the right direction. Traffic is moving along "swiftly" at a 3-mph pace, reaching 5 mph for long periods. After the 405/10 interchange you get out and place a marker to see if you are moving. Hint: turn your radio to 1070 KNX -AM for traffic alerts. Once you get past the 405/101 interchange, traffic will clear and your 5-mph pace will turn to 86 mph in seconds (normal LA driving). Now, where do you eat, sleep, or rest, and still plan on arriving in Lone Pine with time before your hike?

The drive from Las Vegas is somewhat faster, but about the same distance. Reno is another option, which adds maybe 50 miles, but you see many lovely vistas as you travel. From Las Vegas you will drive through Death Valley (which some days reaches 135 degrees) with the option to see if you can make it to the sand dunes and back alive.

Notice the distraction. What may have impacted your experience on the mountain could have started days/weeks before your hike. Things like sleep, drinking, eating, packing and unpacking, or did something get left behind? And the old job ghost... Did you finish the last report? Make the call last week? Tell the bank you are in California? And do you have all your passwords/user names? Charger cords and your special pillow? And that rental car, did you read all the fine print? Not open on weekends, and business hours are 8-5 EST: could mean Eastern or "estimated." And yes, the road service, "I have AAA" (with humor added). The closest rental company is about 75-100 miles away and most often is closed on weekends, so if you run off the road on a Saturday to avoid hitting a rabbit/deer/cow or the other things, the replacement will have to come from 200 miles away.

Now the Hypo's: Over hydration (Hyponatremia, or Low Level of Sodium)

...As in the Latin word *hypo* (below, beneath, or under).

Many references to normal H2O consumption per day seem to be eight glasses of water, while others say three and a half to four quarts a day. Ask yourself, "Do I now review a massive amount of literature on AMS?" Drinking water will not reduce the chance of AMS/HAPE/HACE but one of the suggested methods is to stay hydrated. We are sorry, but after multiple research projects and studies, people will get AMS/HAPE/HACE only if they travel to higher elevation quickly. How high? Maybe as low as 2,000m (we always use m's in America—but for those who aren't familiar, that's around 6,500' or 3.28 x 2,000 meters = 6,560 feet). Well, if you have a real topo map the contours and elevations are in meters (more useless dribble). Many people show signs that may indicate dehydration and exhaustion at any elevation. Drinking sufficient fluids does help one to prepare for the hike. Drugs with different levels of success are available, with various contraindications regarding effect, dosage, and when to start/stop medication (see page 18).

"Made it out sick with incredible strength and determination"
- BOSTON, MA

Think back to your flight. Was the cabin pressurized to 5,000' - 8,000'?

WATER STOPS
Water Stops along the Whitney Trail

All of these water stops are on the Trail. There are several more, but they may be very low or dry.

- **1/2 Mile up the trail:** Carillon Creek
- **3/4 Mile up the trail:** North Fork Lone Pine Creek
- **2 Miles up the trail:** Waterfall area flowing from Lone Pine Lake and Lone Pine Creek
- **2-1/4 Miles up the trail:** Log Bridges
- **3-1/4 Miles up the trail:** Outflow from underground spring
- **3-1/2 Miles up the trail:** Waterfall from Outpost Camp
- **3-3/4 Miles up the trail:** Stream at the northwest end of Outpost Camp
- **4 Miles up the trail:** Outflow from Mirror Lake
- **4-3/4 Miles up the trail:** Above Mirror Lake, entering Trailside Meadow
- **5 Miles up the trail:** Trailside Meadow stream flowing from left of the trail
- **5-1/2 Miles up the trail:** Stream crossing before Trail Camp
- **6 Miles up the trail:** The Poop Pool at Trail Camp (MUST FILTER/TREAT)
- **6-1/4 Miles up the trail:** Small stream without pool above (Cross country and uphill to the north west)
- **7 Miles up the trail:** Switchback 22-25 - Seasonal late June to late August (Ask hikers coming down if they got wet on the switchbacks?!)
- **10.7 Miles up the trail:** Snowmelt just before summit/Keeler Needle—not a reliable source but some years the snow will last all season. You can add snow to your bottle on the way to the summit. Note: only add about half a bottle, then place in your jacket next to your body to melt.

Did you get AMS/HAPE/HACE? Did you have a 50-pound pack on? Or did you walk up and down the aisle, calming other passengers and telling them you are acclimating for your Whitney hike?

We have seen patterns over the years, but there is no controlled study, no proof that any certain thing will work if followed by everyone. The critical fact is this: if you, or anyone in your group, or anyone you find on the trail, has any of the symptoms of AMS/HAPE/HACE, they need to be taken down to a lower elevation. "Taken" means you and/or your group stops, turns around, and takes this person down. That person's life is in danger if left alone. If it is AMS, exhaustion, or other conditions, a person left alone to walk down unsupported may walk off the trail, suffer from a fall or exposure, and expire before located by Search and Rescue. (Watch Dr. Peter Hackett's lecture on altitude illness for more specific info at: www.mountwhitneyforum.com/altitude)

"Down" means at least to the Portal, or where the person can be treated at one of the local hospitals if needed. Many people will recover from the effect of elevation once they reach the Portal (8,365'). But other conditions could still exist: dehydration, lack of oxygen, high blood pressure, or insulin imbalance. A minor injury may require stitches or cleaning; the person may need to be driven to town to be seen by a doctor.

I think your assumption about the hike may be a factor: this is "Everest," or a "walk in the park." Back in 1969, Walt Wheelock reported 20,000 hikers signed in at the Whitney Portal. In 1997, day hikers were added to permit reservation records. Let's assume over the last 30 years we have been here, 15,000–20,000 people start the hike each season. That's an average of 500,000 hikers. Other visitors, let's say 25,000 a season x 30 = 750,000. Add the two numbers = 1,250,000 visitors that have passed through in the last 30 seasons. We've seen enough hikers and visitors to notice the patterns.

These simple steps may help.

> "Has anyone found that lung I lost on the trail?"
> - SAN DIEGO, CA

Arrive several days early—not to acclimate, but to reduce the anxiety factor and relax from your travel. Get a good foundation of the area: find the bathrooms, trailhead, parking, and current weather. Hold group meetings, permit in hand; go over the gear, food, and marching plan. Relax the day before (don't do a hike). Drink a little extra electrolyte and eat a little extra food.

As the trip starts, set a slow and easy pace. Watch the group dynamics; get the slowest hiker to the front early on and make sure that person doesn't push their limits. Try walking behind and distracting the person. When you hear forced breathing, you need to slow down the pace.

Drinking excessive amounts of water may flush out needed elements in your system and can cause hyponatremia or lead to other serious problems while on the trail. So, water alone is a very critical factor to monitor on the hike. Add electrolyte supplements to your water and maintain clear urine. Check your urine color as you hike. Dehydration is a major factor, but the balance of proper water input is also critical.

Hike at a steady pace and refill at each water spot (see page 120). Snack as you walk, drink sips from your bottle, and look around noting landmarks if you need to lead on the way down. Look back often so you know the trail.

Woolpowerus.com offers a 38-page discussion about cold, a very good read for a background if you are not from a cold environment. It explains the body's reaction to loss of body heat and outcomes if not recovered. Please read this article and do more research. Further suggested reading: *Hypothermia, Frostbite, and Other Cold Injuries: Prevention, Survival, Rescue, and Treatment* by Gordon G. Giesbrecht and James A. Wilkerson. My thought is hypothermia is a greater risk than AMS, but they are often combined.

Quick list of some often-quoted information

- Our bodies are made up of about 40 liters of water.
- For normal activity we tend to need 3 liters a day for women and 4 liters a day for men.
- During extreme activity the body can sweat out 1-1/2 to 2 liters AN HOUR.

- Replenishing with only water may reduce your sodium or potassium levels and cause very serious complications.
- The human body likes to be at 80 degrees; this is our natural environment naked.
- At 14,000' you will have 30% less energy.
- At 14,000' the atmosphere pressure is less, causing you to get less oxygen into your system. (The air has the same amount of O2, but less pressure so it can't push as much into your lungs.)
- The body shivers to create heat, four to five times more than at rest.
- Urine color is an easy way to monitor hydration.
- Drink when thirsty. Drink when you feel hungry—this may indicate dehydration.
- Everyone is affected by elevation; very few (20%) are subject to some form of AMS below 18,000' and 50% above 18,000'.
- Dehydration decreases the body's ability to acclimate.
- Avoid caffeine and alcohol before the hike.
- Make a gradual ascent to 10,000' then spend several days relaxing.
- No literature or research suggests ascending to 12,000' from sea level to sleep (in one day).
- After several days at 10,000', a higher elevation can be gained if not overly fatigued.
- Women are often colder than men due to less muscle mass.
- Clothing does not provide heat. It protects your body from heat loss.
- Warm head = warm feet.
- When the body senses cold, it draws into the core, causing the extremities (hands and feet) to give up heat.
- Hypothermic state begins when the body temperature reaches 95 degrees.

- Don't wear metal in cold weather.
- Dry skin is warm skin; wear a base layer that will wick away moisture.
- Breathe through your nose or face guard to save energy in cold weather.
- Loose shoes will help with circulation.
- Cotton can kill (absorbs water and cools the body), unless you are from Colorado and always wore it.

Some Hints
- It is only as miserable as you think it is. Train for a positive outcome.
- You can look at your left foot right now and make it sore or make it dance. The party is your agenda.
- Open neck, vest, jackets and sweaters pump out warmth and take away critical heat from the core.
- Tightly closed neck designs can cause overheating of the core, leading to excessive sweating (water from your system up to two quarts an hour) from heavy activity.
- A light color long sleeve shirt/blouse will keep the sun off your arms.
- A large-brimmed hat will protect your neck, ears, nose, and face (like the saying "redneck").
- Always carry extra socks.
- Soak your feet in the streams to control swelling.
- People affected by exhaustion/AMS/Hypothermia will be pissy.
- Look at the people coming down and ask about the trail/conditions, etc.
- Temperature will decrease 3-5 degrees every 1,000' of elevation gain, unless a major weather system covers an area. Then temperatures may stabilize over thousands of feet. Example: At 10,000' the temperature could be the same as at 14,000'.

- Wind will precede a storm and continue after it. Therefore, when the area is calm, conditions are predictable. And if it is calm and raining or snowing, precipitation will continue until the wind moves the system out.
- When the wind increases, the system is moving in or out and conditions are not predictable.
- Ridge line or down-canyon winds can reach 60-100 mph.
- At about 38 degrees, rain turns to sleet or graupel (snow pellets), and most likely snow will follow.
- Virga is a mass of rain falling from a cloud that evaporates before reaching the ground, usually due to high heat from the ground's surface.
- Zastrugi (or sastrugi) are large columns of frozen snow/ice, caused by wind, creating a vertical column of snow that can impede travel.
- One inch of rain = About one foot of snow.
- One foot of snow can/will drift and cover the Trail above Outpost Camp.
- Systems most often come in from the west.
- Monsoon storms come from the south/east and will have more moisture. Normally these systems may last several weeks.

Some of the information used for this chapter was found on these websites: www.mayo.edu; www.woolpowerus.com.

The Whitney "Trail" in winter.

WINTER

Ok, so if you made it this far in the book, thank you. The thought was to give the reader as much background detail as we could, with examples of what others have experienced hiking the Mountain. We would not be honest if we didn't talk about the shoulder seasons, or as sometimes called, the "dying seasons." These are the months that the trails are covered with snow/ice and no permit is needed for day hikes; or the early and late days of the permit season, roughly May and October.

Note: Between November 1 and May 1, self-issued permits are needed for overnight, and it would be a good idea to place a permit in the drop box for a day hike, just in case. Always leave your trip plan with someone; your life may depend on it!!

Between May 1 and November 1 you have the pressure of getting a permit. Drawing a permit for these early/late months may put you on a trail that doesn't exist, obliterated by snow drifts many feet deep and winter storms moving through the area. You're facing strong winds, very cold temperatures—at times 0 degrees at the upper elevations—and very short hours of light. We always have storms in May and into early-to-mid-June. In the 2018 season we had one on June 10. We had about eight inches of snow in the Portal and drifts of several feet above Outpost Camp. We assume that snow will hit the upper elevation with any storm, and by late August all storms may bring sleet/hail or snow. So, all the discussion up to this chapter brings these topics into focus: your gear, the rubber on your soles, the type of boot you select, what layers of clothing you're wearing, how to protect

> *"When you are the first people out on new snow, taking the time to make switchbacks and cut safe steps is very much appreciated. I am very grateful to those PCT hikers who started the switchbacks leading up the chute rather than just carving a straight line...cutting good steps that are safe for you and others is worth the extra time it takes to reach the top"*
> **- MESSAGE BOARD**

your water from freezing as you hike, and water sources that may freeze along the trail. You may encounter sheet ice on the rocks just before and during stream crossings; you'll need to change the way you walk and protect your eyes from snow blindness. Snow burns from the reflection off the snow surface can be very serious; apply UV protection often. Another critical factor is the ability to calculate how you are doing. Are you able to stay focused on time/distance traveled? Snow travel is slower than walking on a dry trail. Also, if a storm system moves in, can you find your way down in a whiteout? Did the storm cover the tracks you followed or made? Are you ready for the discomfort of blowing snow, and ice crystals forming on your eyelids? Are you prepared for a few slips and falls?

Now, recall the Trail is covered with snow. You see tracks—how do you pick the correct tracks to follow? Will these tracks take you to the bathroom or the summit?? Or, as has happened, off a cliff? Following tracks should be a well-thought-out decision—yes, I know where they go. Yes, if we all stay in the correct track it will pack down and become a safe route, avoiding steep grades or slopes that may have rock coming down from the melt/freeze cycle, and starting slides.

Early one season we had snow covering the area. A couple came in, planning to hike Whitney. Doug Jr suggested they come back once the Trail cleared. "No," the man said, "I retired out of the military and a little snow won't bother us." The next morning, they came in for breakfast and asked for our thoughts. We suggested trying to reach Lone Pine Lake as a test hike, to evaluate ease of route-finding and trail conditions.

They returned later in the day and he said, "We could not find the Trail and even tried having my wife sit on a large boulder while I made a big loop one direction and another loop in the other direction." So, for the next few weeks everyone who came into the store told us it was impossible to follow the trail, it just goes in circles. Be aware of what/whose tracks you are following.

Many outdoor stores will sell winter mountaineering gear. They must assume that you know why you are buying the gear and how to use it. Now on the other hand, if THEY suggest this is what you need... Could this put you at risk? Now the pressure is back on you; do you buy the gear and get the required experience, or ...?

For the experienced winter mountaineers the choice is the Mountaineer's route, for several reasons. The two main reasons are: 1) it is very short, 4 miles vs 11; and 2) the canyon is direct and if snow-covered, a simple ramp takes you up to the notch at 14,000' and then around the corner for the final 500'.

The set-up is, you live in Southern California or a warm zone and your winter may start late in November or not at all. We are sometimes compared to Alaska for the cold and the chance for early snow. If it is in the 70's or 80's where you live, you hike in running shoes and shorts, and you can return to the city in a few minutes, you need to understand that our world is not like that. In the off season (winter) the mountain is very serene, from one perspective. Few if any people are around, and you may need to walk miles for cell coverage or help. The plain hard fact is: YOU ARE ALONE. It will be cold, and it will be dark for hours. I recall a winter where someone was overdue, and I went up looking for the person. Snow was about chest deep on the cold side of the canyon. (Yes, from one side of a canyon to the other conditions can change. On the side getting sun the snow can consolidate. On the shaded side, the snow may stay as ice crystal for weeks.) I would hear clicking noises as I searched, but when the sun would go behind the ridge the clicking noise would stop. My assumption: it was a device that was solar powered. There was not enough detailed information to suggest that the person was in trouble or missing, so Search and Rescue was in limbo on starting a full search. I went up three days and found nothing. Later in the year, several cross-country skiers found his tent and a recovery was started. The clicking sound was never found.

> "There are no guarantees of success in winter and a big storm may well put all of our careful planning into disarray."
> – SIERRA MOUNTAIN CENTER

I will add another example of how the winter weather plays into rescues.

Climbers making their way up the slope to Trail Crest

During a winter storm I got a call about three missing cross-country skiers. Dispatch wanted to know what the Whitney conditions were. I had been in the mountains all day watching the storm move in. I headed down and was able to get on our webcam. I knew what time the storm hit my location, and I was able to relay to dispatch what time the system hit the skiers' area. Luck had it they were very experienced mountaineers and also saw the front moving in. They skied downhill for several miles to gain a lower elevation and skied out west several days later.

Dec. 14, 1974: I knew this young man that thought he could set the winter record on the mountain. He waited till the reports showed sub-zero temperatures, making it possible to stay on the crust from below the campground to the summit at his assumed speed. He carried one Snickers bar and a liter of water, and he wore a light jacket. The reason this person is alive today is that he failed. He fell just above the cable area around 12,500' and knew the area very well. He was able to crawl and fall back to his car many hours later. Pray that you are never faced with that scenario, but plan now for what you need to do if you are. Do you wait and hope the bus comes? Do you assess your injuries and create a plan of action? The experience you bring to the plate when something of this magnitude happens will often determine the outcome, and always circles back to, "If not me, who?"

2
MORE INFORMATION

This section contains supplemental information and is not essential to your success in climbing Mount Whitney. It provides some interesting history and background about the area and can give you great material for a session around the campfire while you're preparing, acclimating, or recovering from your hike.

LIFE AT THE TOP

Celebrations

The top of Mount Whitney is a singular place. Upon reaching the summit, a pause for reflection and self-congratulations is in order. For most people, snapping some photos is enough to mark the moment. However, folks have done more unusual things to commemorate their conquest of the Mountain. A number of couples have become engaged while at the summit. Some have celebrated birthdays, complete with champagne and fireworks. Many cell phone calls have been placed.

We should take a moment to remind all visitors that it is a federal offense to remove ANYTHING from this very special site. If everyone took one piece of anything, it would soon cause deterioration. Please preserve the place for your grandchildren to enjoy when their turn comes to climb Mount Whitney. Besides, you don't want your pack to weigh any more than it already does, so please don't pick up souvenirs.

> "I felt like singing out a thousand 'allelujas. What a tremendous and overpowering feeling it was to know that I was on top of the world, at least here in the continental United States"
>
> - TOM LAROCCA,
>   *THIS YEAR OR NEVER*

Upon reaching the summit of Mount Whitney for the first time, John Muir found a half dollar with the inscription, "Whoever finds this is welcome to it—Carl Rabe" (spelling has been edited). John Muir left the money there, but someone else took Mr. Rabe up on his offer.

Money—you shouldn't expect to need any at the summit, but some entrepreneurial folks have sold hot coffee, beer, and wine for outrageous prices up there. Others have charged $50 for a call from their cell phone. The Guest Book at the Store is replete with comments which jokingly suggest business improvements for the peak: a fast food store, an elevator, a tram, and many more. While there is no zoning atop Mt. Whitney (yet) for commercial endeavors, it has been called "another roadside tourist attraction" along the "hikers highways"—the John Muir and Pacific Crest Trails.

Evidence of civilization has taken to the skies of Whitney in recent years as fighter jets from nearby military bases practice maneuvers over the area. To some hikers, the vapor trails are beautiful to behold, especially when tinted with colors of sunrises or sunsets. Others, however, see them simply as a detraction from the visual environment. Noise pollution is another issue. The roar of jets as they zoom the summit or break the sound barrier is a jarring reminder of the stresses of city life. At times they fly quite low, sending the roar echoing off canyon walls, terrifying animals and upsetting campers who come to the mountains to find some peace and quiet.

While at the summit, hikers are often treated to a spectacular airshow. Some argue that such invasion of the wilderness should be outlawed. Others find it an awesome sight which augments the thrill and excitement of attaining the top of the Mountain.

Sometimes gliders can be seen, soaring like silent giant white birds, hundreds of feet above.

The Hut

The most noticeable landmark on the summit is the stone hut. For today's visitors, the amazing thing about this building is that it was constructed before helicopters were invented. When you think about what you just went through to haul yourself up to the summit, you can appreciate, to a small degree, the task of hauling up materials and completing construction with 1908-1909 tools and technology. This feat, sponsored by the Smithsonian Institution, was performed by Gustave F. Marsh of Lone Pine (See Appendix B, "The Highest House in America," p. 215). He also engineered the early trail to the summit. Fortunately, he had the use of pack animals.

Considering the weather and temperature changes this little building has been exposed to, one must appreciate the quality of engineering and workmanship that went into its construction. Not only has it held up well, it is pleasant to look at. Take a moment to admire its solidity. Mr. Marsh obviously took pride in his work. Dean Prewitt did some restoration work on the shelter for the Forest Service, and the door was rebuilt by Lew Chrispen of Lone Pine. Half the hut is closed to visitors.

Please be respectful of this building; do not use it as an "outhouse," and remember to close the door so it won't fill up with snow. People have used it as a shelter for sleeping on the summit. We do not recommend this.

PLEASE HEED THE WARNING SIGNS ABOUT LIGHTNING!

A hiker was killed in 1990 while taking shelter in the hut during a storm. One other has died at the summit from lightning strikes: Byrd Surby in 1904. If you notice any impending storm activity, hear buzzing or humming sounds, or sense a lot of electricity in the air, DO NOT STAY ON THE SUMMIT! If you are heading toward the hut, do not continue up the trail to the summit if thunderheads are building over the area and people coming down tell you of electrical charges in the air. Lightning is a hazard

"A jet fighter ... came buzzing over us with only a few yards to spare—then climbed up until he was only a tiny speck, and bore down on us in a series of slow rolls, sweeping only 25 feet above the stone hut on the summit, and diving out of sight into the Owens Valley below!"

- BOB BACON

all along the ridge, and even down to Trail Camp. These warning signs generally occur hours before the actual lightning strikes, so you should have time to get down.

Sleeping on the Summit

Each year some people choose to spend a night on the summit. You need to evaluate the pros and cons before you decide to do this.

Pros:
- There is adequate space for camping.
- You will have spent the night on the highest peak in the contiguous U.S.
- You will become closer friends with others who are doing the same thing.

Cons:
- There is no water (unless you gather snow and melt it).
- It is very cold at night, no matter what time of year.
- You probably won't get much sleep.
- If a storm arrives, you'll be in danger of lightning strikes unless you pack up and hike down in the dark—in the rain/snow.
- If any kind of problem develops (hypothermia, leg injury, heart attack, etc.), there will be NO HELP AVAILABLE.

The authors do not recommend spending the night on the summit due to the Cons listed here. However, we realize there is a certain thrill to it, and adventurers will continue to camp out at the top, if for no other reason than to be able to tell their friends about it. All we can say is, be careful, and use "common sense."

| "Slept on Whitney 8/13—fantastic!"
- SO. PASADENA, CA | "Slept on Whitney. Freezing—but the sunrise & set are beautiful!!!!"
- SAN FRANCISCO, CA | "Horrible night on top"
- GROVELAND, CA |

Waterfall at Whitney Portal

The Mt. Whitney Trailhead

The first major stream crossing: North Fork of Lone Pine Creek

Entering the John Muir Wilderness at mile 0.85. You will need a permit to enter the Whitney Zone at mile 2.75 (below).

Log Crossing before Lone Pine Lake

Looking east across Lone Pine Lake

Mirror Lake Cascade

Looking back at Lone Pine Lake from the climb to Big Horn Park

Falls at Outpost Camp

Entering Big Horn Park

Frosty morning at Outpost Camp

Mirror Lake outlet crossing

Mirror Lake from the slabs above

Trailside Meadow

Trail Camp looking south from Wotan's Throne

Snow-covered Switchbacks

Cables on the Switchbacks

View to the west from Trail Crest where you enter Sequoia National Park. The trail on the west side of the crest (below left).

146 — THE MOUNT WHITNEY GUIDE

Looking east through a "Window" between the Needles

Summit Hut at sunrise

Almost there. Hikers approach the Summit Hut

Exposure on the Mountaineer's Route

Pinnacle Ridge from the East Face Route

Storms build quickly on the Crest— know when to retreat!

Bob Rockwell (right) on his 75th birthday summit, November 2010.

And on the summit in 1956. (Photos courtesy of Bob Rockwell)

RETURN VISITS

It is our observation that about 90% of the people who climb Mt. Whitney have what we would call a "spiritual experience." There is something about the area that draws people back again, once they have been here. We have seen people who came to the Portal 20, 30, or more years ago, and are back to fulfill a promise they made to themselves. We also see some of the same people coming back year after year, heeding the call of the Mountain. One older gentleman we know of has climbed it every year, doing it in one day, for many years—an annual pilgrimage.

In 2002, Bob Rockwell commemorated 50 years of hiking and climbing Mount Whitney (in all seasons, including a one-day, ropeless climb of the East Buttress) with his 89th ascent. With over 160 total summits by 2013, along with countless trips on the Trail as a Forest Service volunteer ranger and member of the China Lake Mountain Rescue Group, Bob continues to provide a wealth of knowledge and experience to other hikers and climbers. Here is a list of his milestone climbs:

- **May 24, 1952** — First ascent, age 16 and witnessed a Nevada atomic bomb test from the summit (*See* www.mountwhitneyforum.com/rockwell)
- **August 21, 1956** — First full moon ascent
- **August 1, 1972** — First time up Mountaineer's Route. Took 10-year-old son (10th ascent)
- **December 25, 1973** — Christmas rescue of a climber on East Buttress
- **May 20, 1974** — 12th ascent, 101 years −1 day after Muir's climb of the Mountaineer's Route
- **May 15, 1983** — 25th ascent
- **August 5, 1995** — 50th ascent
- **February 22, 1997** — 59th ascent (had now climbed it in every month)
- **July 13, 1997** — Climbed my age (61st ascent at age 61)
- **April 1, 2000** — 75th ascent
- **December 31, 2000** — Last climb of the old millennium—81st ascent
- **May 24, 2002** — 50th anniversary of first climb, and 89th ascent
- **November 17, 2010** — 75th birthday ascent

Rockwell during the 1973 Christmas rescue of a climber on the East Buttress.

Some people happen by once just to car camp, and then vow to return for the climb. The Guest Book contains hundreds of entries that essentially say, "I'll be back," or "I'm back." Another phenomenon we notice is younger generations of families rediscovering the Whitney Experience of their progenitors. One family visited the Store to tell us this was "Grandpa's Mountain." They had come here to pay tribute to him after he had passed away. We see people with childhood memories of camping here, or visiting a Portal cabin, who have returned to bring their own children and introduce them to the area. Some have even been named "Whitney" after the mountain.

For some people who are sick or physically unfit, Mt. Whitney has provided a goal and a motivation to overcome their health problems. They make a promise to get well, or get in shape, and come back to climb the Trail. A lot of them do. This is one of the rewards of being at the Store, because we usually hear about these personal victories.

We have known of double amputees and polio victims who completed not only the Whitney Trail, but the John Muir Trail. We have seen people who were diagnosed with one disease or another and were not expected to live long. Mt. Whitney has infused them with a will to recover and a determination to climb it before they die. Some of them make it. We have also met older people who climbed the Mountain when they were younger, and have come back to ponder and reflect on the experience. Although most are no longer able to reach the summit, they take satisfaction in the memory of their past climbing experiences.

A lot of people have passed through the area over the years, and each carries unique memories. Some remember working at the store when they were kids. Others remember when the trailhead was at the west end of the parking lot. Many remember when a permit was not required for this trail, and it was climbed by more than 4,000 people on busy summer weekends. Some remember when pack animals were used. One visitor showed us the spot where he was born—in the back of the Store!

Once you have come to Mt. Whitney, chances are you will come back. There is something more than the water, the air, or the granite, that speaks to our inner selves. It seems to cast a spell upon us all, and we are drawn back again and again to renew our spirits. No matter what religion or "non-religion" you believe in, we hope you feel this wonderful "whatever-it-is" and have a desire to return. Be sure to sign in at the Store when you do!

To sum it up: a quote from former cabin owner Tom LaRocca from his account, "This Year or Never" (see Appendix A, page 206) which he wrote in 1979 after his first ascent of Mt. Whitney at age 58:

> *I have often been asked the question: would you do it again? My answer is definitely in the affirmative, for I know now that each time I climb the highest peak in the [continental] United States it will be a thrilling and spiritually rewarding journey. I began with the thought of doing it once in my lifetime—of achieving it being a this-year-or-never-proposition. I know now that climbing Mt. Whitney is too wonderful to remain just a one-time event in my memory. I want to do it again, because I know that each trip will offer different sights, new experiences, and a chance for me to feel once again the awesome power that comes with being on top of the world.*
>
> -TOM LAROCCA, "THIS YEAR OR NEVER," 7/79

Betsy & Jack Northam renew their vows and celebrate their 50th wedding anniversary on the summit in 2018.

A celebration of life for fellow mountaineer Kent Ashcraft in 2009.

SPECIAL OCCASIONS

Climbing Mt. Whitney is a special occasion in itself. However, when combined with another milestone in life, it augments the event significantly. The most common celebration we see is birthdays. If you were born somewhere between June and October, this is one way you can celebrate getting older while staying young. Many people come here for those very special birthdays such as numbers 40, 50, and so on. Standing on the summit gives you the perspective that time doesn't really matter, and that your life is small and great all at once.

We meet a lot of amazing and inspiring people, including those who face serious health challenges. Climbing the Mountain is a significant achievement for healthy folks. A growing number of men and women have done it after a heart attack, amputation, organ transplant, chemotherapy, or other major physical trauma.

We love seeing the multi-generation groups; parents who climb with their children and even grandchildren are creating family memories that will last longer than our tenure.

Wedding anniversaries are often celebrated here too, and vows renewed for the future. One woman climbed the Trail in her original wedding dress, accompanied by her husband of 50 years! Some people meet their "significant other" on the Mountain, and others have come here on their honeymoon.

If you are looking for an exciting way to "pop the question," you might consider proposing on the summit—this will be a story you can tell your grandchildren about, while you climb the trail with them 50 years from now.

Mark Brunke and Gilda Garcia actually got married on the summit. Their wedding took place in July of 1995. This was a very late year for

> *"Aah Hah! I Made it!! And now we're engaged! Yeah!"*
> - REDWOOD CREEK, CA

> *"My b/f proposed to me at Lone Pine Lake," "She said yes!"*
> - PALMDALE, CA

Mark and Gilda got married on the summit (photo from Gilda Garcia)

snow, and the wedding party struggled valiantly to reach the top. At one point the wind even blew the bride over, but they made it to the summit. Gilda wrote:

> Too bad it was so cold because I had a great leopard outfit on under all those clothes. [Above us were] silk Tibetan prayer flags with well-wishes from our friends and loved ones who accompanied us in spirit only. On long expeditions on Mt. Everest, traditionally the flags would be shredded by winds, carrying the messages far.

Mark and Gilda returned to the summit on their 10th anniversary to renew their vows.

Other special occasions that people have climbed Whitney to celebrate include triumphs over bad habits such as drugs, alcohol, or smoking; escapes from bad relationships (by both men and women); career changes; moves into or out of California; and of course, retirement.

There are some life-changing events that aren't always planned but just happen when people make this climb. Couples

A happy 8 year-old reaches the hut on her first Whitney summit.

who were heading for divorce find they can communicate better without all the distractions of home, and their marriages turn around. People without any purpose for living discover the forgotten beauty of a bird, a flower, or the sunrise, and find that life is good after all.

Through the efforts of youth organizations such as Boy Scouts of America, and "Beyond Limits" (a community program that took groups of high-risk youth up Mt. Whitney every year), young people's lives are influenced in a positive way. Kids who were gang members in the city find a new way of life they never could have imagined, and determine to make meaningful changes in their behavior.

We have known people who planned to climb Whitney for one of these occasions but didn't realize they needed permits. Frustrated, they celebrate anyway at the Portal, and vow to return with a permit to climb another time. These promises are often kept.

Unfortunately, some people come to Mt. Whitney to end their lives. A few suicides have occurred during our years here. It is sad indeed to think that even these beautiful surroundings could not give a person hope for something better in this life.

"Tomorrow's my 80th birthday. Celebrating on the trail!"
- LOS ANGELES, CA

"We celebrated our 50th anniversary by going to the top!"
- LOMA LINDA, CA

"The earth in its splendor declares the Glory of the Lord!"
- GERMANY

Looking east over Horseshoe Meadows and the start of the Cottonwood Lakes trail.

A climber on the East Face Route.

OTHER APPROACHES AND LOCAL TRAILS

For anyone planning technical climbs in the Eastern Sierra, we recommend Peter Croft's book, *The Good, The Great, and the Awesome: The Guidebook to the Top High Sierra Rock Climbs*. It includes descriptions of Lone Pine Peak, Keeler Needle, and many others. Two other great climbing books are: *Bishop Area Rock Climbs* by Peter Croft and Marty Lewis, and *High Sierra Climbing* by Chris McNamara and McKenzie Long.

East Buttress/East Face

Only experienced climbers should attempt these routes. Both are currently ranked 5.4-5.7. As with any approach to the summit, altitude and unpredictable weather are variables to be contended with. Your approach is via the Mountaineer's Route, up the North Fork drainage of Lone Pine Creek. This brings you to Iceberg Lake, elevation 12,500' (also known as East Face Lake). From here, both routes ascend the "first tower," from which the East Face route forks to the left, and the East Buttress route heads toward the right. Rockfall is a danger on both of these routes, as well as falling debris from visitors at the summit. Helmets are advised.

John Muir Trail

Mt. Whitney marks the southern end of this 212-mile trail, named after the famous mountain man who helped form the Sierra Club in 1892. The northern end of the "JMT" is in Yosemite National Park. It winds through three national parks, one national monument, and four wilderness areas, following the Sierra crest and passing a number of peaks over 14,000 feet in elevation. We meet hikers who have spent several weeks traversing the entire Trail. More often, people hike short

"Climbed east face, what a rush!"
- GARDEN GROVE, CA

"I made it! John Muir Trail yeah!"
- DORTMUND, GERMANY

segments. A popular route (but one that covers the most difficult part of the Trail) is to enter the wilderness from the Onion Valley Trailhead west of Independence, joining the JMT near Kearsarge Pass. Coming south, the ascent is gentler than the Whitney Trail approach. The JMT turns east for the final climb to the summit of Whitney. A quick descent eastward on the Mt. Whitney Trail ends at Whitney Portal.

People starting the JMT after the middle of August from the south end and crossing over Trail Crest into the back country can be caught by snow. Heading north to Yosemite, conditions can get colder with more snow along the way. Also, in some years the back-country Rangers start coming out in mid-September and the summer resorts start closing due to early snows.

In the last decade the number of JMT/PCT hikers has soared from just a few to thousands. The starting dates are weeks if not months earlier than they were in the late 80's. We think by the end of August, one should be out of the back country or risk having to exit west over many miles. With entry in mid- to late June you can expect ice on the passes. Now we notice many hikers starting the trail mid-May and as late as mid-October. The winter of 2016-2017 delayed many hikers, but it was the run-off that was the controlling element with wide swift water crossings in the back country.

New records are made each year for the trails. At this writing, the record for the JMT is now 3 days 7 hours and 57 minutes. For the PCT, last we heard was 52 days! See fastestknowntime.com for the latest records.

Cottonwood Lakes Trail

For a compromise between climbing Mt. Whitney on a weekend and taking a month or a whole summer to traverse one of the longer trails, this route makes for a meaningful four-to-seven-day wilderness trek. From Lone Pine, drive up Whitney Portal Road approximately three miles to Horseshoe Meadow Road. Turn left, and gear down for the steep drive up to the Cottonwood Pass Trailhead (elevation 10,000'). From this starting point there are several ways to reach Mt. Whitney, giving you about 25 miles of hiking at higher elevations in order to acclimatize for the final push to the summit. All of these trails lead to beautiful Lower Crabtree Meadow. After a refreshing stay there, turn toward the east, following the JMT past Timberline Lake, Guitar Lake, and up the west side of Whitney. You know the way from here. Go to the summit and then complete the loop by descending the Whitney Trail to the Portal.

Pacific Crest Trail

The Pacific Crest Trail (PCT) is one of eight National Scenic Trails. It runs from the Mexican Border near Campo, California, through Oregon and Washington to Manning Park, Canada, a distance of 2,638 miles (4,247 kilometers). The trail follows the "Pacific Crest" along the Sierra Nevada, Cascade, and other mountain ranges. The PCT was created by an act of Congress in 1968, and officially completed in 1993. Many people set off from Campo each spring with a goal to reach Canada by fall. Around one-third of them complete the "through-hike." Most PCT visitors enjoy a portion of the Trail at a time. One of the intersections along this route is the John Muir Trail (JMT) spur leading up to Mt. Whitney. The JMT is a popular segment of the PCT. For those who want a longer piece but aren't ready for the whole thing, you can do 500 miles by hiking around the Lake Tahoe area and then heading south to join the PCT/JMT to Mt. Whitney.

Mt. Muir

Adventurous (and skilled) folks who wish to try something besides the "beaten path" of the Whitney Trail may want to add Mt. Muir to their trip. Along the ridge above Trail Camp, this peak offers experienced climbers a quick side trip that will add another 14,000-plus summit (14,015, to be precise) to their itinerary. It is not a marked trail; do not attempt to climb it if you are a beginner. It is exposed class 3; some say class 4.

> "Done w/resupplying after 130 miles on the PCT—now onto Tuolumne Meadows—then Sonora Pass"
> - PROVIDENCE, RI

Lone Pine Campground to Whitney Portal—National Recreation Trail (NRT)

A lovely little section hike can be found on the south side of Lone Pine Creek by crossing the bridge near the pond at the Portal and turning left. This upper portion of the NRT offers quiet fishing spots as well as house-sized boulders to clamber up, down, and around. In a few minutes, it takes you down to the Whitney Portal Campground. This section of the trail is an easy downhill stroll if you begin at Whitney Portal. From the other direction, it is a bit more strenuous, and is best undertaken early in the morning before the heat of the day. Though this section is only a few miles long, the route covers terrain that varies from flat desert with sagebrush to a cool forest with towering pines and running water. During the 2016 season, The National Recreation Trail was joined by a trail system through the Alabama Hills. So, we joke when people ask, "Can we take a hike?" Yes, from Lone Pine to Canada or Mexico, or just to the road's end. The entire NRT is around 15 miles one way.

Meysan Lakes Trail

The jewel of the Portal area, this trail starts with parking on the Portal Road at the family campground. Unlike the Whitney trailhead, parking is fairly open. From the parking area, go through the campground and cross the bridge toward the cabins. You should see a sign for Meysan Lakes Trail. Follow the trail up through the cabin neighborhood. As it winds somewhat southeast, the trail goes into a canyon where it follows Meysan Creek along the west side. Water is not readily available, and the sun will be on you for most of the trail. Bring plenty of water for the hike up, and refill at the Lakes for your descent.

The Meysan Lakes Trail was rebuilt in the 1994 season and is fairly easy to follow. For the first few miles, a very sandy slope must be crossed, and the trail can be lost in this area. Just keep on the trail to the westerly side of the canyon, off the walls, and continue up to the end of the canyon proper. Several false meadows will be crossed. The final meadow will have a granite ledge system about in the middle of the meadow with a small waterfall running most of the time. Head for the waterfall and you will find the trail up and over this last ledge system. It exits on the bank of Meysan Lake, where you will enjoy great fishing and solitude—a rare find in this part of the Sierra. The hike is about as difficult as climbing the Whitney Trail, so plan a whole day. It's a steep route, traveling 4.7 miles, with nearly 4,000' gain in elevation (from 7,900' to 11,600'). It's ideal if you are staying in the campground and want a very private walk with much scenery. We have found this a great place to hide when Sunday rolls around and we need a "recharge." This canyon also leads you to Lone Pine Peak routes, along with passage to Mt. Irvine and Mt. Mallory. These are not trails and require mountaineering experience.

High Sierra Trail

This is one trail that had little use just a few years ago and now is very popular. It is the right distance for an easy 5-7-day trip covering the back country from the west to the east. Sights include giant trees, giant mountains, rivers, and hot springs. The High Sierra Trail is the trail many are using now for a trans-Sierra hike. There are several entry points and exit points on each side. We tried to get a key pass-off set up, as this is one of the kinks for the hike. It requires two cars or a shuttle; but each season we are closer to linking public transit. It is now a one-day bus trip to go north from Lone Pine to Reno or into Yosemite, joining the Yosemite Area Regional Transit System (YARTS) at Mammoth. Or, catch the bus south to Lancaster where you can either take the Greyhound to Bakersfield or the Metrorail into Union Station Downtown Los Angeles.

Backcountry Exploring

Many cross-country treks can be reached from the Portal area: Arc Pass, Whitney Pass, Crabtree Pass, Vacation Pass, Tulainyo Lake, Wallace Lake, Sky Blue Lake, and on into the back country. We get calls all the time

> "Tulainyo Lake...starkly beautiful at 12,802' a.b.s."
> - CLAREMONT, CA

Meysan Lakes Basin

for details on "can this [route] be done?" Most of the time Doug Jr. or Sr. have done the trip, in the Whitney backyard. HOWEVER—this doesn't mean you should "get a poke and a pickle" and off you go. We have found many times that what looks like a good canyon or chute on the west side of the range will turn into vertical terrain at the top, or vertical on the east face. A review of the early literature mentions great disappointments as these first ascents were attempted.

We want to emphasize that any cross-country travel is not hiking. It will always require technical climbing skills and advanced map reading skills. What looks good on the map will almost always turn into steeper terrain than you expect. We go very light, bringing only a day pack and climbing gear, and have had to travel most of the night on several trips to stay warm and get home with our tails between our legs. Depending on the time of year, storms can make passing from the west side to the east side very dangerous. Several feet of snow can fall in a short time, covering the trails over the pass at Trail Crest.

Indian Encampment on the Carillon Mesas
by
Marcyn Del Clements

Now the night wind
wakes in the foxtail pines,
and they begin to sing
as a Sturgeon Moon
rises in the south,
rises straight up Lone Pine Peak.

I didn't seek out this solitude
but here I am,
alone on an alpine fell field.

I talk to myself. I talk to my stove.
Every time it fires up on the first match,
I praise it. You sweet thing, I say to it.
I talk to the marmot—
he pretends to be stone.
I talk to the ants that
carry off my fallen crumbs.

If I said I talk to God,
it wouldn't be a lie.
Up here—there's just the fox pines,
the meadow flowers
and the turning stars.

—*Previously appeared in "Newsnet," St. Ambrose*
  Episcopal Church Monthly Newsletter,
  December 2001, ed. by
  The Rev. Canon Douglas Edwards, Rector

Morning sun strikes Whitney and the Needles.

THE MOUNTAIN

Mt. Whitney is the highest peak in the continental U.S., and is located in the Sierra Nevada Mountain Range in California. At an elevation of 14,508 feet, it is not a summit to be taken lightly. If you have traveled through Owens Valley on Highway 395, you have passed through its shadow. You may not have noticed its majestic presence. A shy mountain, Whitney rises west of the highway, camouflaged among other mountains of similar size and shape. It is not visible from any other main road.

You can get a closer look at the mountain by turning west off 395 at the only stoplight in Lone Pine, and heading up to Whitney Portal. If you drive up in the winter, you'll be stopped by snow and gates before you reach the parking lot. But, if you come in the summer, by driving only 13 miles off the "beaten path," you'll discover a hidden canyon full of beauty, adventure, and a wide variety of interesting people with stories to tell. This microcosm is the closest you can get to Mt. Whitney by car. There are two options for getting closer: a day hike or backpacking (see first section for more information).

Horses and pack animals are used in parts of the High Sierra back country, but are no longer allowed on the Whitney Trail. The story is told of one such animal who suffered an untimely death on the Trail some years ago. The packers had no time or inclination to properly dispose of it, so they rolled it a short distance off the trail. As days went by, complaints filtered down to the Forest Service regarding a moldering carcass on the Mountain. They got upset and ordered the store owners, who owned a pack outfit at the time, to get rid of the thing. "Don't worry, we'll take care of it," was the reply. And so, they did—their dynamite blasts removed all

"Magnificent! I'll be back to climb someday!"
- HERMOSA BEACH, CA

"I'll get in shape and return!"
- SILVER SPRINGS, MD

traces of the remains! A similar incident was reported in 1996 on the back side of Whitney.

When you get to Whitney Portal, tilt your head back and look up. This should keep you occupied for a few minutes and reward your decision to explore. Depending on the weather and the time of day, you may see the sun, the moon, stars, clouds, falling snow, satellites, fighter jets, or experimental aircraft overhead. Mt. Whitney is still hiding in the distance, but its neighboring peaks and ridges already surround you. The hypnotic spell of steeply-cliffed granite beckons you to come higher. Most people who visit Whitney Portal for the first time make a vow to come back. As the Guest Book testifies, many of them return, one, two, or twenty-five years later. This is a mountain that leaves a lasting impression.

Elevation of Mt. Whitney

Each season we have numerous reports on the elevation of Mt. Whitney. Various maps, books, gift items, and common knowledge range anywhere from 14,491 ft. to 14,508 ft.

To establish the elevation of a point or place, certain things have to happen:

1. There needs to be a base datum
2. Different methods or procedures can produce varied results
3. Adjustments of the data are returned corrected for known errors
4. Results are published based on final adjustments

Benchmarks are classed by order of procedure to establish predicted results. Some common maps show VABM. This stands for Vertical Angle Benchmark, meaning trigonometry methods were used to establish elevation. This is not a bad way to establish rough elevation within one to three feet, but cannot be considered for adjustment into a network because of large probable error.

Another method for establishing rapid elevations is to use an aneroid barometer based on local datum, usually adjusted to the local airport barometer. Again, results are reported to the nearest foot. In the past, this was acceptable for the most common use of the findings, which was map making for base maps.

Precise levels can only be reached by measuring the difference of elevation forward and return to the same point. This method provides a check on each benchmark established. Since the only factor is difference of elevation, the base datum can be adjusted, and all benchmarks can then be corrected. Now—what about movement between benchmarks? This is very real in California, and any states that have crustal motion and sudden movement. Real elevations only exist for the instant they are recorded. Some areas are very stable, others are not.

The published elevation by the U.S. Coast and Geodetic Survey based upon the sea level datum of 1929 reports the first order elevation of B.M. (benchmark) 14,501 ft. This was adjusted in 1940 to 14,494.164 ft. Vertical control, as well as horizontal control, for the United States is now maintained by NOAA (National Ocean and Atmospheric Administration). To get an elevation for a benchmark, visit www.ngs.noaa.gov, or contact:

National Geodetic Survey, SSMC3 #9340
1315 East-West Highway
Silver Spring, MD 20910-3282

NOAA has readjusted the base datum for the United States. We contacted their office and established if California was to be reported, what would be the correction for Mt. Whitney. It was determined by NOAA that the run through Owens Valley would show a +3.45 ft. to the known elevations. Therefore, a correction to the last published elevation of Whitney would be 14,494.164 + 3.45, establishing an elevation of 14,497.614 ft.

We hope this clears up any concern about the elevation of Mt. Whitney. The disks on the summit report several different elevations. Think of these elevations as names for

"The mountains are wonderful"
- VIENNA, AUSTRIA

The trailhead is generally easy to find. (Photo by Richard Piotrowski)

the point, and contact NOAA for the current true elevation. Here is a link to the data sheet for Mt. Whitney: **mountwhitneyforum.com/ngsdata/**

Please explore the www.ngs.noaa.gov website. They have just posted a section to explain the new adjustment, with the results being published in 2022. This will establish a reference datum. The model they show will reduce the local area by .75 meters. What they use now as a base point for the existing Benchmarks will probably be the controlling factor, or they may do a complete adjustment and calculate all new heights. You can research heights here too.

THE PORTAL

A few years ago, one campground host responsible for emptying trash and cleaning fire rings used to shovel all refuse, including hot coals, into the back of his pickup truck. By putting slats around the bed of the truck, he increased its capacity and decreased his number of trips down the hill. On more than one trip down the narrow, winding road to Lone Pine, smoke billowed from the heap. While the people at the Portal were aware of the problem, it took several trips before the poor fellow realized he was driving a truckload of fire down the hill to the dump.

There are four campgrounds, a fishing pond, a picnic area, two trailheads, and a cluster of summer cabins in the Whitney Portal area. The Meysan Lakes Trailhead is on the left of the road about 1.5 miles before the end. Just past this trailhead is the Whitney Campground, which contains 44 sites for car camping, four rest rooms, and some great fishing spots along Lone Pine Creek. Immediately west, at the next turnoff, is a small campground with three campsites for larger groups, such as scout troops, family reunions, etc. Farther south, across the Creek, are some private cabins, perched on a slope above the campgrounds. The next turnout on the left is the overflow parking lot, designated for backpackers. More parking spaces can be seen along the left side of the road.

At this writing, there are four pit toilets at the Portal. Two are in the day parking area southwest of the pond and are only open during the season (May through October). Two are at the main trailhead. These two might be open in winter, but bring mountain money (TP)...and they may be snowed closed.

Several years ago, a truck was pumping out the tanks when someone thought they smelled and saw a human body, or parts of one, in the muck. With some alarm, they asked the Store People to summon the Sheriff. After a great deal of hubbub and poking about, the analysis was made. Some visitor had stuffed a jacket into the latrine. The garment became inflated with gas and waste, giving it the appearance of a torso. In addition, someone else had cleaned a deer and disposed of the entrails in the toilet. The blood and guts made a terrific smell, and a colorful decoy. Everyone was greatly relieved that an autopsy would not have to be performed.

The Ravine campground was built during the 2014 season adding 10 more walk-in campsites. This campground is just below the overflow parking lot and is quieter and more private than the trailhead camp sites. Staying at the Ravine campsite will add about a 300-foot walk to the trailhead, but the advantage is you only unload once. Your car will already be in the parking lot and food in the storage boxes at that lot. This saves loading your stuff up at the family campground, then unloading again when you drive to the trailhead. Staying in the Ravine or trailhead walk-in sites solves a lot of problems. If you stay in the family campground, the other campers may be disturbed in the early hours of the morning as you load up for the trail. Also, you could be taking a site from a family that might not have interest in hiking Whitney but just want to car camp for a week-long trip. Staying one night at this site can cause more work for the camp host who has to clean the sites after each one-night use.

Bulletin boards with information about bears, weather, Forest Service Regulations, and messages to/from hikers mark the Whitney Trailhead on the right. This is the "jumping-off spot" where people launch their Mt. Whitney climbs. Likewise, returning hikers end their treks here, wearily casting off backpacks and boots as they celebrate their accomplishments with sighs of relief. Many hikers actually forget items that they take off when their hike is finished, leaving them at the trailhead area (boots, packs, jackets, poles, etc.).

One day a backpacker came into the store and asked directions to the trailhead. He was told to go back down the road about 20 steps, where it would be easily visible. A few minutes later he returned for more information—he hadn't been able to find it. Once again, he was directed toward the trail. When he returned for the third time, the storekeeper firmly advised him that he should reconsider his plan of hiking the mountain. If he couldn't find the beginning of the trail, he was a pretty high risk for getting lost on the way to the summit.

A little farther along the road, one sees the miniature fishing pond on the left, and the Whitney Store on the right. A few words about the pond: Over the years, and with the weather changes, the pond has shrunk in size and is now almost completely gone. It is rarely stocked during the season by the Department of Fish and Game. They vary the days so fishermen won't plan their trips around its arrival. Licenses are required for all those over 16. The Whitney Store does not sell fishing licenses; you can buy them in Lone Pine.

The pond has a wooden platform where wheelchair-bound visitors can cast their lines comfortably. Unfortunately, some folks are rather possessive about their fishing spots. Contrary to what people may tell you, there are no special privileges granted to those who have fished the pond before.

One hot afternoon, an avid fly fisherman threw a cast out into the pond and immediately felt a bite. He began to reel it in, when he heard a loud outburst of Spanish expletives from a woman who was fishing across the pond. At once he realized he had snagged her entire catch, a stringer with five trout languishing in the shallows. After he pulled it in, he returned it to the woman, and they had a good laugh.

The picnic area is found as the road curves left around the west and south edges of the pond, where day parking is available. Near the junction of the road loop lies a small campground designated for backpackers only. These 15 sites are nothing more than tent pads designed to provide a one-night-only sleeping spot for hikers passing through.

One attraction here that often goes unnoticed is the beautiful waterfall cascading down the southwestern cliffs of the Portal. We estimate the lower falls at approximately 300 feet. Combined with the upper falls, this Lone Pine Creek runoff tumbles a total of 500-600 feet, making it one of the tallest falls in the Eastern Sierra.

> "Rarefied"
> - **VERMONT**
>
> "I climbed to the top of the waterfall!"
> - **VENICE, CA**

A typical high-season afternoon at the Store. (Photo by Richard Piotrowski)

Just what the doctor ordered.

Earlene especially loves the little resting spot at its base, where she finds refuge from the store crowds. One day a group of drummers performed at the top of the lower falls, sending their rhythms echoing off the rock walls throughout the area.

The waterfall grows and shrinks during various stages of runoff. In the cold weather it quiets down, freezing into beautifully shaped icicles. Although its constant rush is a soothing sound, the increased noise of heavy melt off sometimes keeps folks awake at night. The falls can usually be seen from the road—a shining white ribbon.

THE STORE

The Store's original cabin structure of 480 square feet was built in 1935. Bruce and Grace Morgan operated the business for over 20 years (from the 1940's to the 1960's), which included pack trains. The building was used as living quarters, with the store operating out of the front room. Doug remembers one day when someone came into the back (now the kitchen) of the Store to point out the spot where he was born.

During the 1950's, regular pack train clients included Hollywood director Billy Wilder, who enjoyed escorting movie stars on one- and two-week trips into the backcountry. Since the ban on pack animals, the Store has changed hands several times, with various adjustments in product offerings, facilities operations, and management styles. The structure has been remodeled a number of times. After an avalanche destroyed the back of the building in 1969 it was repaired and enlarged. The most recent improvements were made in 1997, giving the store an updated appearance and increasing its size by several hundred square feet.

The way we look at it, the Whitney Portal Store has a mission: to serve the people who come in. We sell lip balm, bumper stickers, and sandwiches, but this place is different than a typical convenience store. The range of clientele covers all socio-economic levels, and literally reaches around the world. Serious climbers choose protein bars and electrolyte-replacement drinks. Car campers shop for matches and marshmallows. Backpackers purchase wool socks and water purifying tablets. Cabin people buy postcards. Day hikers and tourists scoop up T-shirts and refrigerator magnets. Unshaven folks

"Nice feast after the mountain"
- **ENUMCLAW, WA**

"Caught my first fish"
- **SANTA CLARITA, CA**

"Nice people/good conversation"
- **WEST GERMANY**

coming out of the wilderness hungrily order a hamburger with "real fries," a soda or beer, and a shower.

Aside from the wide variety of products and services the Store offers for sale, there is another commodity exchanged: human contact. People need to be alone sometimes, and that is often the reason they come to wilderness spots. But the need for someone to talk to and share mountain experiences pulls them back to this non-threatening mid-point between civilization and the woods. The Whitney Store is a great place to "hang out." Tables and chairs on the patio invite visitors to stop and chat with each other. The indoor stools were removed after one customer "hung out" for six hours, however. One of the few rules at the store: be considerate of your fellow customers—take turns!

Another attribute of the Store that you may not find at your local junk-food mart: willingness to help in an emergency. Danger is very real on this mountain, and many customers have come in needing help. The Store has functioned as an emergency shelter, a hospital, and a rescue station. This service was not in our original plans, but when crises happen, we do what we can. Of course there are many needs we cannot meet.

One spring day, a bus coming up the road to the Portal broke down. The 18 Romanians on board walked the last couple of miles in freezing snow and sought shelter in the Store. None of them spoke English, but it wasn't difficult to tell what they needed—hot drinks! The front part of the Store was hardly larger than an elevator, but all were invited inside where they purchased coffee, tea, and soup while drying and warming themselves. Then it started to hail, and the crowd was augmented by several campers who came up to get protection from the pounding stones. Somehow room was made for them too, and for three hours the Store looked like one big party with over 30 guests. The hail ended; a replacement bus arrived; the Romanians were bussed down the hill; and the campers went back to their tents. Such is life at the Whitney Store.

The daily flow at the store:

Where's the bathroom? The Trailhead? I am here to get my permit! One member of our group didn't come down last night, we need to start a rescue. I have a reservation for site 7196 at Horseshoe Meadow and I'm meeting the packer in 15 minutes. Can I see Whitney from here? Someone is locked in the bathroom! When will they stock the pond? My cell phone doesn't work, what time does the shuttle come? Can you call me an Uber? I need the LA Times for the game scores. Did you see my buddy? He was in here yesterday with a backpack and a blue shirt asking about the bathroom and trailhead. Tell them I'm from the group that's lost, I'm down now. Can you get someone to go up and get our gear? The storm came in so quick we just went to the summit and left our gear. Excuse me, but the line is long—just put me on a burger. We heard someone yelling help. The weather report said…! I have AAA. Someone stole my pack. Is this the road to the big trees? Am I walking uphill or downhill? How do I get out of here? How much further up does this road go? Can I drive to Mt. Whitney? You must be wrong! I have coordinates that say pick up your permit here. I lost my cell phone/wallet/keys/pack/jacket/favorite hat/poles/friend. Do you have my shirt? I lost it here two seasons ago.

I want a grilled cheese with no bread. My husband said he would be down at 4:17, we need to start a rescue. I can't find my kids. Someone broke my windshield/back window. Did anyone else see that in the sky? Just call a helicopter to get my group, they are tired and hungry. Where is Fred? You say they just left him?!

We notice that many people have stopped 27 other places and asked the same question! What is the weather forecast? What time should we start? Do we need axes or crampons? I am taking 7 liters of water. Most often our

"Perfect & fine service!!!"
- **CHOMUTOV, CZECH REPUBLIC**

"Thank you for the shelter"
- **ROTTERDAM, HOLLAND**

"The pancake was breathtaking (and the mountain wasn't bad either)!"
- **LAGUNA NIGUEL, CA**

Becky, Mya, Cayden & Doug Jr.

answers are different from others. We are committed to giving the most current information. We don't want to sell you gear and talk you in or out of going. We have just learned over the past 30 years that we can answer many questions based on what has and what can happen. We have talked with thousands of hikers and visitors that return with the experience they had. We have watched many people reach the summit accomplishing a lifetime goal. Maybe not on the first attempt, but the second, third, or seventh. Others are returning with new friends to do the hike.

We lived in the Portal for 25 seasons, talked to a few bears, watched many sunsets and sunrises, observed the deer as they walked by, shoveled some snow, and walked the 50 feet to work. Most years Doug Jr. would return from another season of skiing, park his camper, and live in the Portal with us. He was set up at the top of the stairs, a great location for the night questions... I can't find my car, trailhead, or someone didn't come down. He spent many nights helping people out. In 2000 he bought a house in the Alabama Hills; he now does most of the supply runs and is the morning person. Doug Jr. and Becky married in 2004 and started a family. Now they have two children, Cayden and Mya.

Our grandson, Cayden, came with Doug Jr. almost every day when he was younger, and we would hike around, exploring the area. Some days were spent fishing or just hanging in the Store. As Cayden got older, we worked on many National Trails Day events, and other trail projects in the Portal and the Alabama Hills. In one of the early years we were traveling cross country and came upon a bear fishing in the stream. We watched each other for a while and moved on. Doug Jr. and I had climbed quite a bit when he was growing up, so Cayden was next in line.

Nowadays the motorcycles, fishing, and school are the focus. We go out in the winter on mountain bikes to ride in the Hills, and take a few ski trips when we get snow. Doug Jr. taught Cayden to ski at a very young age. Mya and Becky do the sledding around home. Doug Jr. and Cayden built a 4-ski sled using a golf cart roof and attached the skis to the bottom. It uses a pipe for steering control and braking system. We have slid two miles down Hogback Road. The Portal Road is too steep, but 4-6 miles is possible in a good year.

Cayden receiving a conservation stewardship award from the Bureau of Land Management, with Doug Sr. (left)

Doug Sr., Cayden, Earlene and Doug Jr. in the Portal kitchen. (Photo by Shin Namura)

Just the right size.

RECIPES FROM THE WHITNEY PORTAL KITCHEN

One day a gentleman came into the Store and asked a question. Doug Jr. thought he said, "Where's the rest room?" so he gave the standard answer: across the pond. A few moments later, the man returned: "Not the rest room—the Restaurant!"

If you've eaten at the "Whitney Store & Restaurant," you'll know that the Store IS the Restaurant. In fact, when we bought the Store, we didn't even realize there was food service involved. When we discovered our new business included a restaurant, we adapted by learning and creating recipes that worked well.

Cooking for guests at 8,300'+ altitude has its challenges. Earlene laughs about it now, but she was near tears when one of the Store's first cooking catastrophes happened. A customer ordered fried eggs for breakfast. Earlene heated up the griddle, and cracked open a fresh egg. The minute it hit the metal, the yolk broke. She tried again, with the same outcome. After going through about 15 eggs, she was desperate. The customer was wondering why his eggs were taking so long to cook. Doug gave it a try, with the same explosive result. Finally, they explained the problem to the customer. Shrugging, he said he'd just take them scrambled.

After puzzling over the phenomenon, it was discovered that subjecting an egg to the temperature change (from very cold to very hot) at the high altitude was simply more stress than the yolk's membrane could bear. This explains why eggs "sunny side up" are not part of the breakfast fare.

For a time, the restaurant's clientele came chiefly from the local towns, but the Thompsons eventually changed the menu to appeal more to

> "Never had such a nice breakfast"
> - HOLLAND

campers and hikers. This also simplified their challenges of keeping adequate supplies on hand. The kitchen is open seven days a week during the season.

Most visitors eat at the outdoor tables, since indoor space is limited. The atmosphere and scenery outside outdoes any restaurant you've ever visited before, unless the weather is bad. The menu is small, but the food is unbeatably tasty, and portions are large enough to satisfy any hungry mountaineer. We've included a few personal favorites; most are no longer served in the store since we simplified the menu, but you can try them in your own kitchen for a delicious homestyle meal.

For some of these recipes, you might not need your measuring spoons or cups. All you need is a sense of adventure—have fun!!

Doug Jr.'s Pancakes

We make these BIG (average is 12-17 inches across). One per person is usually plenty—they are very thick and filling. This recipe makes ONE.

The store will let you have them for free if you can eat a whole one. The record is three pancakes at one sitting.

We started a tradition with our pancakes to help out young families who couldn't afford an expensive meal. We would challenge them to eat a whole pancake, and if they could finish it we wouldn't charge them. We then tailored the size of the pancake to the size of the family—trying to make it big enough to fill them up but not too big that they couldn't finish it. We even had a T-shirt for a while that said, "I ate the cake," for anyone who could eat the whole thing.

> Approx. 4 cups Krusteaz Pancake mix
> Vanilla extract
> Ground cinnamon

Add warm water to consistency of muffin mix (very thick). Do not overmix; should be lumpy. Pour in vanilla until consistency is a bit thinner, but still thicker than cake batter. Pour in cinnamon. Cook on oiled grill or skillet at about 350 degrees. Flip once, use a tooth pick or cut to check for doneness. (Flipping more makes the surface stiff.)

A Little Bit Different French Toast

This makes four servings.
8 slices of bread—sourdough or wheat is best for this recipe.
4 eggs, whipped
A splash of orange juice
Cinnamon
Nutmeg
Vanilla

Combine eggs, orange juice, cinnamon, nutmeg and vanilla in a bowl. Coat both sides of a slice of bread. Cook on oiled grill or skillet until brown on each side. Repeat.

Earlene's Chicken Breast Marinade

Open your spice cupboard wide for this one!

2 cups orange juice
1/4 cup honey
1/2 cup barbecue sauce
1 onion cut into large pieces
3 large cloves
Crushed garlic
Fresh fruit pieces: orange, lemon, pineapple

Combine all ingredients in a bowl. Pour in herbs and spices of your choice—use your imagination and your nose! If you need some suggestions, try oregano, sage, Worcestershire sauce, and tarragon. Start out sparingly—you can always add more.

Lightly puncture chicken breasts, marinate in mixture. We use frozen, skinless chicken and this recipe will marinate a lot. You may want to divide large portions of chicken into Ziploc bags, add a cup of marinade, and keep it in your freezer.

Defrost in the fridge before grilling, sautéing, or baking (may also be broiled). Always cook chicken until meat is white at the thickest part and the juices are clear. Place some of the fruit pieces on chicken while it is cooking for a real treat. Cook as fast as possible so it doesn't dry up, but be sure it's done all the way through.

Doug Sr.'s Special Mountain Corn

These ingredients sound odd together but give it a try—you'll be surprised!

- 1 large can of corn with liquid
- 1/4 cup honey
- 1/2 teaspoon cinnamon
- 2 tablespoons margarine or butter
- Dash salt and pepper

Cook slowly until the water evaporates. Serve as a side dish.

Prime Rib

- Prime Rib Roast
- Garlic
- Salt
- Pepper
- Lemon Pepper
- Worcestershire sauce
- Pesti's Italian Spaghetti Seasoning

Turn meat skin side up. Poke several holes and put 1/4 clove garlic into each one. Pat on salt, pepper, and other spices. Best cooked in a kettle barbecue approx. 3 hours for a whole prime, but use a meat thermometer to be sure. Oven method: roast approx. 3 hours at 325 degrees, or until meat thermometer indicates 155 degrees in center of largest area for about an hour. Ends should be well done and center cuts will be medium to medium rare.

Barbecued Turkey

- Whole Turkey
- Salt
- Pepper
- Sage
- Onion
- 2 cups Orange Juice
- Worcestershire sauce
- Butter or Margarine

Lemon Pepper
Pesti's Italian Spaghetti Seasoning

Wash turkey inside and out with cold water. Empty cavity, remove neck and giblets; save for soup (see next recipe). Salt and pepper inside cavity, sprinkle with sage, and place a whole, peeled onion inside along with the orange juice. Splash Worcestershire. Butter outside of bird and sprinkle with salt, pepper, lemon pepper, and spaghetti seasoning. Cook in a kettle barbecue: 2-1/2 hours for a 12-pound turkey. We always use a meat thermometer to be safe: 170 degrees (internal).

"Don't Throw That Carcass Away" Soup
If parts of carcass are burned, break off and discard.

Salt & Pepper
Turkey Carcass, Neck and Giblets you saved
1 large Onion
4-5 Celery Stalks (with leaves)
4-5 Carrots
1 can Corn (drained)
2-3 large Potatoes
1/2 cup Tones brand chicken or turkey gravy mix
Celery salt
1/4 lb. pasta

In a large pot, cover carcass 2/3 with water. Add salt, pepper, neck and giblets. Bring to boil, simmer partially covered about one hour. In the meantime, chop onion, celery, and carrots into bite-size pieces and keep in cold water until broth is done. Chop unpeeled potatoes, parboil in salted water, and set aside. When broth is done, take out all meat and bone. Carefully remove meat from bones. We prefer to discard neck and giblets (and our dog prefers that too!). Add vegetables and meat to broth. Mix small amount of cold water into gravy mix and add to soup to thicken. Season soup with celery salt, pepper, or anything you like. Break pasta into 2-inch pieces, add to soup. Simmer about an hour. Add more Tones if it needs more flavor. Enjoy!

A mule team heading down the Whitney Trail on the west side of the Crest. (Photo from the Eastern California Museum)

A BRIEF HISTORY

First Ascents and Place Names

The claim to Whitney's first ascent was hotly debated for a few years, along with its rightful name. The peak was actually named Mount Whitney in 1864 when it was discovered (but not climbed) by a field party of the California Geological Survey, which included William Brewer and Clarence King. The men called it the "culminating peak of the Sierra," and named it after Josiah Whitney, who was a Professor at the California Academy of Sciences, and founder of the California Geological Survey (in other words, he was their boss). King tried twice to climb it on this trip, but was unsuccessful. He returned in 1871 to try again, and believed he had reached the summit on this third attempt. So did everyone else, for a time. This "false Mt. Whitney" that King climbed is at the headwaters of Tuttle Creek, several miles south of the real Mt. Whitney, and is now known as Mt. Langley.

The three men who made the first ascent of the "true Mt. Whitney" were Charley Begole, Johnny Lucas, and Al Johnson, reaching the proud peak at noon on August 18, 1873. These residents of Lone Pine climbed the peak as a diversion, and were dubbed the "Three Fishermen." It doesn't take much imagination to see the irony in this story. Poor Mr. King craved the first ascent so badly that he tried three times, exhausting all of his supplies, to reach the summit. When he finally thought he had accomplished the feat, he had actually climbed the wrong mountain. (Because of the cloudy weather, he was unable to see the higher peak to the north.) When his error was discovered two years later, he hurried back to California from the East Coast to try once again. He climbed the real Mt. Whitney on September 19, falling into

> "To him [Marsh] more than any other one man is due the successful completion of the trail and the building of the observatory"
> - A. MCADIE, U.S. WEATHER BUREAU

The unpaved Portal Road. (Photo from the Eastern California Museum)

fourth place in the contest. Besides the three fishermen, two other parties reached the summit before King.

Residents of Owens Valley wanted to name the mountain "Fisherman's Peak" to pay homage to the first climbers. They certainly felt closer to these three local friends than to Dr. Whitney. When this was challenged, they proposed the name "Dome of Inyo." Over the next two years, the local newspaper published many articles arguing this issue. Finally, a bill which would make "Fisherman's Peak" the official name was introduced in the State Legislature. A strange twist of fate brought the bill before the Senate on April Fool's Day, 1881, where they frivolously amended it to read "Fowler's Peak." The Governor ended the silliness by vetoing the bill, and so today the original name stands: Mount Whitney.

John Muir made his first ascent of Whitney on October 21, 1873, just a month after Clarence King finally reached the summit. Muir tried the southwest approach, as all had done before, but ended up dancing all night among the needles to keep from freezing. He returned to Independence where he refreshed himself, and then made his way up the east side, the first to do so. His course roughly followed what is now known as the "Mountaineer's Route," along the North Fork of Lone Pine Creek.

Other early climbers included a student, a photographer, and in 1878, a group with the first four women to reach the summit. One of these, Miss Anna Mills, is described as being "lame," and may therefore lay claim to the first ascent by a person with a disability.

The first overnight stay at the summit took place on September 2-3, 1881. Captain Otho E. Michaelis, along with two or three other members of an expedition, camped on the west side and hauled a tent and a quarter-cord of wood to the top. The wind was so fierce they could not put up the tent, and their campfire burned all the wood long before the sun came up. Like many others since, they did not get any sleep during their night on top of Mt. Whitney. This party, led by Prof. Samuel Langley, consisted of several professors and scientists who were interested in the unique opportunity for scientific observation that this peak offered. Its level area on top, and the abundance of stone for building material, led to the suggestion that a permanent shelter be constructed on the summit.

Who Built the Trail, and When?

Various groups worked on the beginnings of a trail to the summit of Mt. Whitney, including the Buffalo Soldiers U.S. 9th Cavalry, Troops I and M; and several local parties. The lack of supplies, plus the rigors of winter storms, stopped them from reaching their goal.

The original trail from the east side to the summit of Mount Whitney was completed by the community of Lone Pine under the leadership of Gustave F. Marsh on July 18, 1904. Mr. Marsh was also responsible for completion of the summit shelter in 1909 for the Smithsonian Institution. This rock house was used for scientific observations in 1909, 1910, and 1913, and stands today as a notable landmark. (See Appendix B, page 215.)

Authors' Note: We are extremely grateful to George Marsh, grandson of Gustave F. Marsh, for the material included in this chapter. He has shared generously from his own research, including biographical information on Gustave, and the history of Mt. Marsh.

Summit Shelter with Telescope, 1916.
(Photo from the Eastern California Museum)

Horace Elder cleaning snow from hooves of "Mattie" on top of Mt. Whitney in a snowstorm.
(Photo from the Eastern California Museum)

Gustave F. Marsh
Builder of the Trail and Summit Shelter

Gustave was born in England in 1869, came to the US in 1890, and became a citizen in 1902. He first became acquainted with mountaineering by working in the mines in Colorado. Other work brought him to Owens Valley where he met and married Elizabeth Dodge in 1901. They settled in Lone Pine, where he took over the local U.S. Mail route, and also carried Wells Fargo Express and passengers. He designed a local water system in 1902, and built southern Inyo County's first telephone line in 1903. He became thoroughly committed to the improvement of Lone Pine and the surrounding area. It was his goal to make Mount Whitney a significant asset to the community. Gustave was quick to realize that it could become important to scientists and tourists. Because he was a newcomer in Lone Pine, it took him several years to convince the community to take action.

He worked hard to raise funds and volunteers to build the trail. When the first team ran out of money and

> *"[It] reflects very high credit on Mr. Marsh and his supporters that the trail was ever completed"*
> – **C. G. ABBOT,**
> **SMITHSONIAN INSTITUTION**

Original cairn at Summit. (Photo from the Eastern California Museum.)

motivation, Marsh raised more cash and led a fresh team for a second assault in 1903, finishing the trail in 1904. Charles G. Abbot of the Smithsonian Institution wrote, "Under the leadership of G. F. Marsh the trail was completed to the Summit. Funds were scanty, and it was only by the greatest economy, pluck and perseverance that Mr. Marsh succeeded in getting the trail to the top."

Professor J. E. Church, University of Nevada, persuaded Marsh to accompany him on a winter climb in March of 1905. They spent eight days trying to gain the summit but were turned back by avalanche conditions at approximately 13,500 feet. From a letter Marsh wrote to Church in 1930:

> You remember when we went over Whitney Pass and the whole mountain started down, it sure did not feel so good. And then walking in that deep soft snow and to come under that great comb of snow hanging over us. How we tried and shoveled and tried again and how you said we are taking our lives in our hands every five minutes, so I said we had better quit. I wish you could have seen that place when the snow was gone. It would make you shiver."

Gustave's interest in meteorology resulted in contact with Professor Alexander McAdie, Chief of the U.S. Weather Bureau Office in San Francisco. McAdie, who had recommended Mount Whitney for a weather observatory, was notified of the completion of the trail. He subsequently recommended Marsh to Dr. William W. Campbell, Director of the University of California Lick Observatory on Mount Hamilton. (Dr. Campbell later became President of the University of California (UC) System.) A serious plan to build a shelter on the summit

> "...this station...is everything that I could have hoped to find, and more; but existence is only possible on the summit with permanent shelter, for though at the moment I viewed it it was calm, yet the wind and cold would be fatal to life at other times, without house and fire."
> - 8/24/1881, S. P. LANGLEY

Oscar Bernhardt and mules in front of the summit hut. (Photo from the Eastern California Museum.)

began to form. Gustave accompanied Dr. Campbell and C. G. Abbot, Director of the Smithsonian Astrophysical Observatory, to the summit in 1908, where they decided to construct the shelter. At this time, the trail was in need of repair and improvement to accommodate the transport of materials and instrumentation to the summit. Before the project could be started, Marsh was required to commit that the trail would be in good shape at no expense to the Smithsonian Institution.

Gustave Marsh donated much of his own time on this project and was paid only for the hours spent building the shelter. He worked tirelessly day and night, staying on the summit while others descended to rest or retreat from storms. He is credited with making Mt. Whitney available to science, as for many years the hut was the world's highest astronomical and atmospheric study station.

Abbot recorded,

> Marsh worked at all kinds of jobs himself—cooking, breaking stone, carrying stone, carrying snow for water, riveting and cementing, as well as general bossing. He will never get paid in this world for the work he did on that house.

Dr. Campbell reported,

It [the Mount Whitney shelter] is a great credit to the Smithsonian Institution and to the superintendent of the construction, G. F. Marsh, a public-spirited citizen of Lone Pine, who struggled valiantly and successfully against the difficulties of transporting cement and steel to the summit, as well as difficulties of less open character. Marsh's connection with the project is one in which he is entitled to feel the utmost pride...."

Marsh's own words, in a 1930 letter to Prof. Church:

During the time of putting up the building I stayed on top 43 days. I had 15 men to start with and only 5 at the finish. We had a terrible thunder storm when we were almost done. Our cook was knocked down by a flash of lightning at 9 o'clock one night and another flash almost finished us all. But the storm passed in a few minutes. Leaving all jagged points of rock and squares on the sand screen and the fuzz on the ropes one mass of lights. St. Elmo's Fire, we did not know what it was. So you can guess how scared we was. I urged the men to work fast so as to get done and get away. When next day at about 5 P.M. we heard muttering of thunder way over towards Arizona and the clouds rolled up the mountain just as the sun went down. I wish you could have seen those clouds in red suns [sic]rays, If Hell was ever turn loose it was in those clouds. I told the men to get under cover and we would be alright. But one by one they ran down the mountain and left me alone. So I went to bed and covered up my head, like a kid, till the storm passed over. I was alone 3 days. Then the men came back and we was glad all around. Prof. Abbot came up a few days after, just as the work was done. I got everything completed 24 hours ahead of time and $250.00 below my estimate. So I was happy....

Modern-day visitors may not be impressed by the sight of this humble house. Some assume its parts were flown in by helicopter. A better appreciation for its solidity can be felt when one realizes the task was undertaken without modern conveniences. Water was obtained by melting snow. Wood and cement were hauled up by mules. Stone was broken, shaped, riveted and cemented with hand tools. All this hard labor was performed at an altitude where oxygen is scarce and temperatures vary drastically. Amazingly, the whole project was completed in a little over one month, for about $5,000. (See Appendix B for a feature news article published in 1909, "The Highest House in America.")

Several scientific expeditions soon took advantage of the stone hut. In 1909 Dr. Campbell returned with others, bringing a 16" horizontal reflective telescope and a spectroscope. They were able to end a significant controversy by determining that no water vapor existed in the Martian atmosphere.

In May of 1910, Gustave went to the summit of Mount Whitney alone, as no one would go along. He checked to see how the shelter had held up through the hibernal harshness, and retrieved the temperature data recorded during the past winter.

McAdie wrote:

> I received a telegram from Mr. G. F. Marsh, of Lone Pine, saying that he climbed Mount Whitney and reached the summit yesterday (May 23, 1910) and found our instruments left there last August all right. He gives the lowest temperature on the top of the United States proper last winter as 23 degrees F below zero and the highest, 57 degrees F.

Gustave had another reason for summiting on this particular date. It was a unique opportunity to observe Halley's Comet and a total eclipse of the moon, and he did not miss it. He had the best unaided view of both events in, at least, the entire United States. Marsh was up most of the night as he watched the moon darken with the earth's shadow. Suddenly the comet appeared, larger than expected, quite bright, and very beautiful. Eventually it dove into a fog bank to the west, with the tail streaming behind. (See Appendix C for Marsh's own account of this remarkable experience.)

Mr. Marsh repaired the trail in 1913 for a Smithsonian expedition that studied nocturnal radiation from the summit. In 1926, another study took advantage of the conditions on Mt. Whitney to observe the earth's cosmic rays.

Marsh raised his three children in Lone Pine, where he continued to be active in the community. It seems he never wasted any time or material. He served on the school board of trustees for 16 years and as a County Supervisor for one term. He was totally committed to the future of Lone Pine, and he thought it was the loveliest place in the world. He enjoyed the view of Mount Whitney during the day and stars in the clear sky at night for his 46 years there.

Gustave is given credit for two sayings, one from his son Gus: "Nova rich, they blew it before they learned to spend it." And the other from G. P. Putnam: "Englishmen you meet seem to be going home. Americans appear always to be on their way to the office."

MOUNT MARSH

In 1937, Chester Versteeg named Mount Marsh in honor of Gustave F. Marsh. Versteeg wrote, "G. F. Marsh, of Lone Pine, California. Builder of the first trail to the summit of Mount Whitney from the east in 1904 and the builder of the Smithsonian Institution shelter house on its summit in 1909. The Englishman who fought prejudice, high altitudes, the jagged Sierra Crest, desertion, the elements—but finished the job."

The first ascent of Mount Marsh was completed on August 25, 1940, by Chester Versteeg, Andy Hennig, Bob Rumohr, and John Wiggenborn. Unfortunately, the record of the peak's name was lost to history for a time.

Mr. George Marsh, grandson of G. F., sustained a persistent effort toward gaining recognition of the name, Mount Marsh. His efforts were finally rewarded. The U.S. Board on Geographic Names (USBGN) made the name Mount Marsh official on January 10, 2002. Mt. Marsh is located above Consultation Lake just north of Mt. McAdie.

> "The comet was in plain view as soon as it was dark & just before the moon was covered [by the eclipse] ... the tail almost reached the moon, it swept almost across the [entire] sky."
> - GUSTAVE F. MARSH, JUNE 5, 1910

Mt. Whitney from late 1800s Lone Pine.
(Photo from the Eastern California Museum.)

Lone Pine

As more people came to visit Mt. Whitney, more accommodations were built. The original Whitney Portal Road was constructed in 1933-35, making it possible for tourists to drive their automobiles up from Lone Pine into the lush little canyon. Public campgrounds, picnic areas, a store, a tract of summer homes, a pond, and a potable water system were all planned and built in the 1930's, making this area more accessible to the general public.

The summit shelter was restored during this period by the National Park Service. Cabins were built and rebuilt up through the 1940's and early 50's. The Whitney Portal Road was rebuilt in the 1960's. Other more recent improvements have included the addition of overflow parking lots, and the upgrading of campgrounds. Today's emphasis is not on improving the facilities at Whitney Portal, but on preserving them. Overuse of the fragile Mt. Whitney environment has made it necessary to limit the number of visitors through a quota system of permits. The historic Mount Whitney pack trains, originally part of the Portal Store operation, have been eliminated as well. People are welcome here, but must be willing to take their turn—by waiting for a trail permit, reserving a campsite, or standing in line at the Whitney Store.

The lifeline to Owens Valley is Highway 395, which runs north and south through this mystical plain between the White/Inyo Mountains and the Sierra Nevada. The mountain ranges rising on either side of the Valley provide the most dramatic scenery to be had in the area. Bishop is the largest city along this route, and lies about 60 miles north of the road to Whitney Portal. Heading south from Bishop, Big Pine is the next dot on the map, followed by Independence, and finally Lone Pine. Each of these little towns has its own personality, and its particular landmarks.

It takes less than five minutes to drive through Lone Pine. There is only one traffic light in the town. Nothing about its appearance belies the colorful history it holds. Even the tree it was named for has disappeared, washed out in a flood.

The first white residents built a shelter on Lone Pine Creek in 1861. More people came to raise crops and livestock, building homes of adobe. The earthquake of 1872 destroyed most of the buildings, and killed 27 people. Nearby mines soon brought a transient population mixing Mexican, Welsh and Cornish immigrants. The town slowly grew, its patch of green widening as citizens planted orchards and fields of alfalfa.

The Carson & Colorado Railroad, running through Owens Valley, was completed in 1883 in hopes of a rich commerce with local silver mines. Among these mines was the Cerro Gordo, atop the Inyos due east of Whitney Portal. This was the southernmost of the famous Comstock Load, from which the Hearst family derived its initial wealth.

The ups and downs of silver prices, along with the inconsistency of the area's mines, took local settlers through economic extremes of prosperity and hard times.

One of those who helped bring new life to the Valley was Monsignor John J. Crowley, a Catholic priest who

> "Laughter is as important as food and drink and the shirt on your back."
> - MSGR. J. J. CROWLEY

served in this parish in the 1930's, after serving as Chancellor of the Diocese of Fresno/Monterey. A dedicated and hard-working man, the "Desert Padre" began his typical day with a 6:00 a.m. mass in Death Valley. Leaving at 7:00 a.m., he drove from below sea level up and down two mountain ranges, arriving in Lone Pine to perform the 9:00 a.m. mass. This ended at 10:00, when he would race north to say mass at 11:00 a.m. in Bishop. Msgr. Crowley became known for the wear and tear he put on his automobiles.

An important goal the Padre worked toward was to unite the people in his parish—not just Catholics, but all men, women, and children—and to instill a sense of pride in the community. The downtrodden residents had become bitter over their past losses, and Father Crowley brought them reasons to smile again. A jovial soul, he organized street carnivals and local plays. He formed the Inyo Associates, a Chamber of Commerce of local editors, miners, farmers, and merchants. Cutting through an atmosphere of mistrust and intrigue, he joked his way into their hearts. He saw a vision for the future of this desert valley in its potential for tourist attractions. He also knew there was a water shortage.

Father Crowley proposed that a dam be built to the north which would ensure adequate water for Owens Valley residents as well as thirsty Los Angeles. He wrote columns about the Valley, lectured about it in Los Angeles, and drew newspaper reporters and photographers with his unusual publicity tactics.

One of these was a special mass at the top of Mt. Whitney, which attracted the attention of people all over the country. Another was a "Fishermen's Mass," said at three a.m. on the morning of the first day of fishing season. The Father invited all fishermen of all religions, along with the media. His little church was packed with Valley friends who happily listened to his three-minute sermon discussing Jesus, the greatest fisherman. This tradition of a "Fishermen's Mass" carried on for a number of years after his passing.

Another press event was staged by the Padre to promote a new road joining the lowest point in the U.S. (Death Valley) with the highest (Mt. Whitney). The Wedding of the Waters began as Indian runners filled a gourd with pure, icy water from the

Father Crowley blessing a young girl's fishing pole for success. (Photo from the Eastern California Museum)

nation's highest lake (Lake Tulainyo) just below Mt. Whitney's summit. The gourd was transported in turn by pony express, burro, covered wagon, mule team, railroad car, and airplane. Finally, it was sprinkled from the airplane into Badwater at Death Valley, the lowest body of water in the U.S. News of the two extreme points involved in this fascinating ceremony spread all over California and beyond. Tourists began to pour into the Valley, bringing dollars and economic growth never before experienced by the sleepy little town of Lone Pine. A re-enactment of The Wedding of the Waters was put together By Huell Howser for his popular TV show, "California's Gold," in 1999. You can watch it here: www.mountwhitneyforum.com/huell

The area of Whitney Portal continued to attract more visitors, and a tract was surveyed for 30 cabin sites. Father Crowley began construction of his own mountain home on one of the plots, overlooking Lone Pine Creek and the Valley he loved. Unfortunately, he was killed in an auto accident shortly after the cabin was completed.

Eventually the dreamed-of dam was built north of Owens Valley, and the lake it formed now bears the name of the fondly remembered Father Crowley.

BIBLIOGRAPHY

Abbot, C. G., "A Shelter for Observers on Mount Whitney," *Smithsonian Miscellaneous Collections (Quarterly Issue)*, Vol. 52, Part 4, No. 1886. Washington, DC: Smithsonian Institution, January 12, 1910.

Bard, Allan, "Mt. Whitney: 14,495 Ft., East Buttress III, 5.7," *Shooting Star Guides*, Bishop, CA (undated).

Chapman, Robert D. and Brandt, John C., *The Comet Book: A Guide for the Return of Halley's Comet*. Boston: Jones and Bartlett Publishers, Inc., 1984.

Englander, William R., "Conquering the mountain in a day," *The San Diego Union-Tribune*, May 20, 1993.

Farquhar, Francis P., *History of the Sierra Nevada*. Los Angeles: University of California Press, 1965.

French, Harold, "The Highest House in America: How the New Observatory on Mt. Whitney Was Constructed," *San Francisco Chronicle*, November 7, 1909.

Giesbrecht, Gordon G. and Wilkerson, James A., *Hypothermia, Frostbite, and Other Cold Injuries: Prevention, Survival, Rescue, and Treatment*. Second Edition. Seattle: The Mountaineers Books, 2006.

Graham, Tom, "The Drama of Mt. Whitney," *San Francisco Chronicle*, August 10, 1992.

Harris, Kamala, "Honoring the dedication and courage of the Buffalo Soldiers." S. Resolution II, Senate of the U.S., 115th Congress 2nd session, Feb 16, 2018. www.harris.senate.gov/imo/media/doc/021518%20Buffalo%20Soldiers%20Resolution.pdf

Hellweg, Paul and McDonald, Scott, *Mount Whitney Guide for Hikers and Climbers*. Canoga Park, CA: Canyon Publishing Company, 1994.

Houston, Charles S., M.D. *Going Higher: The Story of Man and Altitude*. Revised edition. Boston: Little, Brown and Company, 1987.

Inyo County Search and Rescue, "How to Get Help." inyosar.com/how-to-get-help/

King, Clarence, *Mountaineering in the Sierra Nevada*. Lincoln, NE: University of Nebraska Press, 1970.

Langley, S. P. "Researches on Solar Heat and Its Absorption by the Earth's Atmosphere," U.S. War Department, Washington, DC: Government Printing Office, 1884.

Lone Pine Chamber of Commerce, "Lone Pine: Home of Mt. Whitney & Lone Pine Film Festival," January 1996.

Marsh, George F., "Gustave F. Marsh & Mount Whitney." Laguna Woods, CA: Personal research compiled and revised 22 December 2000.

Marsh, Gustave F., Letter to W. W. Campbell dated 5 June 1910. Archives of the Lick Observatory.

Michelson, Megan, "Whitney Has Turned Into an Overcrowded Catastrophe," *Outside Magazine*, August 9, 2018. www.outsideonline.com/2330916/mount-whitney-climbing-accidents

National Park Service, Division of Publications, *Sequoia and Kings Canyon: A Guide to Sequoia and Kings Canyon National Parks California*. Washington, DC: U.S. Department of the Interior, 1992.

Perez, Mary Anne, "Troubled Teen-Agers Weather Inhospitable Climbs," *Los Angeles Times*, August 14, 1991.

Putman, Jeff and Smith, Genny, ed., *Deepest Valley: A guide to Owens Valley, its roadsides and mountain trails*. Mammoth Lakes, CA: Genny Smith Books, 1995.

Roeser, Marye, "The Role of the U.S. Cavalry in Building the Mt. Whitney Trails in 1903." American Mule Museum, 2019. www.mulemuseum.org/building-mount-whitney-trails.html

Rowell, Galen, "The John Muir Trail: Along the High, Wild Sierra," *National Geographic*, Vol. 175, No. 4, April 1989, pp. 466-493.

Sierra Mountain Center, "Mount Whitney in Winter." www.sierramountaincenter.com/tours/mt-whitney-in-winter/#all

Spillman, Benjamin, "It's a long way to the top of Mt. Whitney," *Reno Gazette Journal*, October 22, 2015. www.rgj.com/story/life/outdoors/recreation/2015/10/15/s-long-way-top-mt-whitney/73832528/

Stone, Irving, "Desert Padre," *The Saturday Evening Post*," May 20, 1944.

Taliaferro, Charles R., *Mount Whitney Hiking Guide*. Independence, CA: High Sierra Adventures Trailhead Shuttle Service, 1986.

Thompson, Doug, Jr., "Lone Pine Area Virtual Tour 2015." YouTube Channel: Whitney Portal Hostel & Hotel. 15 Nov 2015. Web. 17 Nov 2018. www.youtube.com/watch?v=BnSgx-5qQiM.

U.S. Department of Agriculture. Forest Service. Inyo National Forest. "Eastern Sierra Visitor Center." Web. 15 Nov 2018. www.fs.usda.gov/recarea/inyo/recarea/?recid=20698.

Wheelock, Walt and Condon, Tom, *Climbing Mount Whitney*, Fifth Edition. Glendale, CA: La Siesta Press, 1989.

Whitney Portal Store Guest Book, 1989-2018.

Whitney Portal Store Message Board. www.mountwhitneyforum.com.

Wood, Crispin Melton, "A History of Mount Whitney," Unpublished Thesis, College of the Pacific, 1955.

APPENDIX A

THIS YEAR OR NEVER
by Thomas A. LaRocca
August, 1979

Authors' Note:
The authors chose to publish this personal account by Tom LaRocca for several reasons. Even though it was written nearly 40 years ago, the experience is timeless enough that it still portrays a "textbook" example of a typical Mount Whitney experience, in that it describes the mental and physical preparation Tom went through before attempting to climb; it includes good examples of the interactions between hikers that take place as they move along the trail; it gives a clear schedule of events, including the time of day things occurred; it mentions some experience with altitude sickness; and it expresses emotions that most climbers feel as they undertake, conquer, and descend the peak.

We express our gratitude to former cabin owners Tom and Wilma for their generosity in allowing us to share this writeup with you.

This is my sixth year at our Whitney Portal cabin. I cannot count the number of times I have focused my sights and attention on the majestic and breathtaking peak that is Mt. Whitney. And each time I would ask myself the questions: Will I, and can I, climb to the top of Mt. Whitney?

I had heard many stories throughout the years of rescues made by helicopters and rescue teams, not only during the cold months, but also during the warm season. I had seen and talked with many hikers who had just finished their long trek. Mostly they had looked tired and had little to say. Some just couldn't wait to have a hamburger or an ice cream cone. And of course, I had heard the stories of many successful hikers.

Will I, and can I, climb to the top of Mt. Whitney, the highest peak in the continental United States, 14,495 feet? I had to find out. I made my big decision. This was the year, 1979, that I would attempt to do it. Now that my decision was made, there were more questions: What would be my strategy? How would I prepare myself? Knowing that I had to condition myself both physically and mentally, I set out to do this. And I worked hard at it. It is important to mention at this point that I wanted to make the climb and the descent in one day—a real challenge. Could I do it? I didn't know, but I had to find out.

Early in the season I hiked up the Meysan Trail alone—once in May and again in June. I didn't go very far—only to the first big waterfall (about two miles) and back. This was a good start in my conditioning process.

I don't like to hike alone, so I was fortunate in finding good hiking companions, new owners of a neighboring cabin, to accompany me on practice hikes. On Saturday, July 7, we started out to explore the Whitney Trail. Although we did not set out with any destination point in mind, we did rather well. We went as far as the five-mile marker—Consultation Lake—returning home after seven hours. It was a good exercise in preparation, and we felt none the worse for it. I slept well that night and had no aches and pains the next morning. I hiked that day in Hush Puppy ankle boots, which I found to be light and supportive. They worked well for me.

Two weeks later, July 21, the three of us made our second climb up the Whitney Trail. This time I wore jogging shoes, which didn't work too well. I slipped while crossing a log. Luckily my foot was not injured—just very wet. This was hardly a deterrent, so we continued until we reached the six-mile marker at Trail Camp. We had gone one mile farther than our last hike, and we all felt strong. We knew that we had the stamina to continue on, but turned back downhill to attend a dinner we had been invited to that evening at another cabin. I was a bit tired, but slept well and felt fine the next morning.

I was fortified with the thought that if I was able to hike six miles up the Whitney Trail, why not eight miles, or even farther?

I had high aspirations. After a trip back home to Alhambra Hills, I received a call from another friend and fellow cabin resident who had heard of my goal to climb Mt. Whitney. He had been jogging ten miles every night for a month to get into shape, and suggested a plan to do the big climb on Thursday, August 3. My practice hiking partners were not available on this date, so the two of us made arrangements to take a short hike on Tuesday, relax on Wednesday, and go the full distance on Thursday.

On Thursday, July 26, the day after my 58th birthday, my wife and I headed for the High Sierra once again. My friend arrived at the Portal Monday evening, July 30. Our practice hike on Tuesday was a steep scramble up the slope behind the cabins, where we reached one of the lower ridges after two and a half hours of fighting loose gravel. This was a great workout for our leg muscles. While we had planned to relax on Wednesday, we ended up helping haul a load of fir bark, pushing a wheelbarrow back and forth for part of the day. Again, this strengthened the muscles we would use the next day.

After a good dinner that evening, we planned what to wear the next day: long trousers, long-sleeved shirts, wide brimmed hats, and sun glasses. My friend decided to wear his hiking boots, and I went with my personal favorites, my Hush Puppy ankle boots. I went to bed early that night, full of anxieties and with that ever-present question: could I reach the summit of Mt. Whitney? I did not sleep well, suffering from stomach cramps. I had mixed feelings about this, but in the end I convinced myself that this distress was all for the better, since I would not have the cramps in the morning.

When the alarm rang the next morning at 3:45, I got quickly out of bed, feeling alert, happy and anxious. My stomach was fine. I ate a light breakfast of orange juice, puffed wheat, coffee, toast, and jam. I quickly packed my lunch: a sandwich, fruit, nuts, and candy. I walked down the hill to my friend's cabin, arriving at 4:45. He was ready, frisky and in good spirits. His Father drove us up to the foot of the trail, where we set out at 5:05 a.m. At long last we were on our way—and none too soon.

We were forced to use our flashlights the first ten minutes on the trail, but that was hardly an inconvenience. We found, to our surprise, that we were not the only ones on the trail at that hour, for we saw two young damsels several yards behind us. Were they in distress? By no means—they looked and acted as if they knew where they were coming from and where they were going. They were moving fast and traveling light. Our acquaintance with these young ladies turned out to be a fortunate event, as will become evident as this story progresses.

At the beginning of our climb I found myself perspiring and gasping for breath. This continued for about two hours. I began to be concerned and was forced into some unpleasant reasoning: if I'm off to such a bad start, what will be the outcome? Will I eventually have to turn back? It seemed best not to let such doubts bother me. I did not make my feelings known to my companion. He could have moved at a much faster pace, I am sure, for he is taller, long-legged, and strong. He was sympathetic and kept up a pace which I could follow as he humored me along.

We encountered overnight campers at Lone Pine Lake, the first of the lakes along the Trail, about two and a half miles from Whitney Portal. They had just awakened and were moving about. We stopped to chat, and then moved on. At this point, I got my "second wind" and felt revitalized. The air was crisper and cooler. Feeling more comfortable and in a good state of mind, I took the lead position. We exchanged the lead position at will throughout the entire hike.

We arrived at Mirror Lake—10,000 feet altitude—at 7:30. We had completed the first four miles, and I would venture to say that they are the easiest for two reasons: first, it's a dirt trail up to this point; secondly, the grade isn't quite as steep. From Mirror Lake on it's granite rock all the way to the summit and the climb becomes steeper and more difficult. In spite of these hazards we did not slow down or stop for breath. Our young lady friends passed us along the way—I don't remember exactly at what point—but I would guess it was somewhere after Mirror Lake. Before they passed, we conversed with them and learned they were from Illinois and were presently students at USC. My friend borrowed their suntan lotion, after which they proceeded on their way.

We arrived at Trailside Meadow at 8:15. This is the five-mile mark. It's quite pretty, with little purple flowers scattered along the streams and small birds begging for crumbs. We rested here for a few minutes and drank several cupfuls of ice cold running water. How refreshing it was!

We continued our steep climb and arrived at Trail Camp, 12,000 feet altitude, at 9:15. From here we could look down into Consultation Lake, the biggest of all the lakes on the Whitney Trail. From this viewpoint it looked cold and uninviting. There was no ice or snow around it, however. We saw campsites, colorful tents, and hikers milling about—a very impressive sight indeed!

After leaving Trail Camp came the true test. I had hiked to this point once before with my friends—all well and good. Could I surpass my previous mark? I was certain that I could. I felt strong and sure-footed. The next two miles were the well-known—perhaps more accurately termed infamous—one hundred switchbacks. Are there really a hundred of them? I don't know, but someone must have counted them. We were well above timberline now, and all we could see around us was granite rock and big patches of snow alongside the switchbacks. I had no problem climbing these; neither did my friend. Water was plentiful in this area, with streams passing over and under the Trail.

Before long we could see the top of the ridge, but we were still a long way off. I was becoming very anxious. My friend kept my spirits up by telling me that it was just a matter of minutes. We then met a very weary hiker, which gave us an excuse to stop, rest, and chat. We learned that he was just starting his three-week trek. On his back was a sixty-five-pound pack! He took out a cigarette, lit it, and then breathed a sigh of relief. He remarked that he would not smoke while hiking. This young man has passed through my thoughts many times since, and I have wondered if his three-week trip was a success. He seemed unprepared mentally and physically for such a long journey. We wished him God-speed and left.

At approximately 11:00 a.m. we arrived at Trail Crest Pass, 13,777 feet altitude. The view now was breathtaking, beyond description. For the first time we could see the other side—the western slope—Sequoia National Forest. We decided that this was the place to have lunch, since there was plenty of atmosphere and scenic beauty. The winds were a bit strong and gusty, but it didn't matter. I made a feeble attempt at eating. I really wasn't hungry, but managed to eat half a sandwich, a tomato, and a small bunch of grapes. This satisfied me. My friend, on the other hand, was famished and ate two sandwiches. We rested awhile, and soon realized that an hour had passed. It was noon and we still had two and a half miles to go.

The next half-mile was easy, for it was all downhill—a kind of misleading introduction to what was to come. In about fifteen minutes we reached the John Muir Trail Junction. Here we ran into (not to be taken literally) about six hikers coming up from Sequoia, from whom we learned that another hiker from Sequoia was in trouble on the trail below. The best we could gather was that he needed assistance and that a friend was helping him carry his pack. We could see them coming up the trail ever so slowly. In the meantime a hiker—and a good samaritan indeed—was heading down the trail. He was trying to get word through that someone was in trouble. Not until later was this episode resolved for us.

At the Junction I started out before my partner. This was a mistake, for I took the wrong trail. It would have taken me into Sequoia National Forest. Then came my friend's loud question: "Where do you think you're going?" I turned around and followed him, as he chided me a bit. We had now covered 8.7 miles—just another two miles to go. Could I do it? I knew I could. I felt good and strong. According to my hiking companion, this was the part of the journey where you walk fifty yards and stop to catch your breath. He wasn't far from wrong, even though he had exaggerated somewhat. When he got too far ahead of me, I would shout out to him, "Remember your words—every fifty yards we stop—right?" And we would both chuckle as he good-naturedly waited for me.

About a mile before the summit we began to pass hikers who had reached it and were making their descent. We came across a troop of boy scouts—some looked no older than nine or ten—and some looked ill. The altitude had taken its toll. As we moved closer still, we could see the two pinnacles beside Mt. Whitney. As we passed on the trail between them, I had all I could do with keeping both feet on the trail and keeping myself balanced. It was a sheer drop on both sides of the trail. I found this portion of the trail to be dangerous and treacherous, and we were crossing it in the most ideal of conditions.

The back side of Mt. Whitney has an entirely different appearance than the front. It is well-rounded, whereas the front side is pointed and jagged. My friend kept up his words of encouragement to me, and tried to point out the stone house at the summit, but I could not see it. A pair of hikers who passed at this point must have seen the weary and forlorn look in my eyes. They encouraged me with their smiles and their comment, "You're there now!" These words gave me new vigor. We pushed on and finally arrived at the stone house at 1:40 p.m.

Yes, the hour of glory and fulfillment had come. I felt like singing out a thousand 'alleluias. What a tremendous and overpowering feeling it was to know that I was on top of the world, at least here in the continental United States.

It is customary that one sign the register outside the stone hut. This I was very happy to do. I asked my friend to take a photo of me standing by the register. Another climber nearby overheard this request and offered to take a picture of both of us by the register. I hoped that this shot especially would come out.

After the signing in we advanced straight ahead, toward the side facing Whitney Portal and the Owens Valley. Soon we realized that our young lady friends had made it up before us. As we sat and chatted, they mentioned that one of them had been ill on the way up and was still feeling queasy. They left the summit to make their descent at 2:15. We were destined to meet these girls one more time later on.

We planned to spend an hour or more on the summit, leaving at 3:00 p.m. This would give us ample time to absorb the majestic beauty of Mt. Whitney's peak. As we sat facing the Owens Valley, munching grapes, tiny birds flitted about after the seeds. I was surprised to see these little beggars at this altitude.

After awhile, my partner stretched out under a long rock to avoid the sun and took a nap. I, on the other hand, started a conversation with the same gentleman who had snapped our picture by the register. He was very informative, and happy to explain what we saw before us—peaks, passes, lakes, and forests. He knew the country well. This is easy to understand, for besides being an experienced teacher, he was also a scouting coordinator who had hiked the High Sierra for a good many years.

Time was moving along; already it was 3:15. It was time to make our descent, but my friend was nowhere in sight. I searched for fifteen minutes, calling out his name. Naturally I began to wonder about his disappearance. Horrible thoughts passed through my mind—had he fallen off a ledge? I saw a stone enclosure in the distance which aroused my curiosity, so I walked over in its direction. It had no roof. As I approached, I could see an opening. With a sigh of relief, I found him inside.

Needless to say, he had fallen victim to the altitude. I sympathized with him. He took two aspirin and then courageously expressed a wish to move on. We were somewhat behind schedule, but we knew we could make up the time on our descent.

After two hours my companion was feeling better. His fast pace told me as much. After a mile or so down the trail we saw a rescue helicopter overhead. We knew that it was not just passing by, that it was definitely searching for someone in distress. Immediately we concluded that it had to be the person needing assistance back at the Junction. About three hours had passed, and we were now heading down the switchbacks. The helicopter continued to weave in and out of our mountain range. It was very interesting to watch the pattern of its flight. We had to wonder if at any point it would land, and finally it did. We were about three quarters of the way down the switchbacks when we saw the helicopter on the ground at Trail Camp with several people alongside it.

We arrived at Trail Camp about 5:30. By that time the helicopter had already taken off and returned to its base. The best information we could gather was that the person supposedly in distress had not wanted to be flown in for medical aid. He claimed he could make it on his own. We discussed the high costs of flying in a chopper these days, and who would be obligated to pay for this service.

As we made our way through Trail Camp, we observed lots of

activity. Here was a small community—about thirty or forty hikers—young and old, busily moving about. Tents had already been pitched, stoves were burning, and some hungry campers were already eating their evening meal. Everyone was high-spirited and, I'm sure, anxious for what was to come the following day. We were greeted with big smiles as we passed through, and found it easy to chat with some of these campers.

We still had six more miles ahead of us, but fortunately it was all downhill. This was very consoling. We quickened our pace and at times went into a running walk. We kept this up till we reached the end of the trail at Whitney Portal. It was now 8:20, and somewhat dark. For me, thirst was more of a factor than anything else. The first thing I wanted was a cold soda pop, so we stopped at the Portal Store.

Continuing on, we soon heard welcome voices from the parking lot. Once again it happened that two gentlemen met the two damsels—who were <u>not</u> in distress. This was providential. The girls remarked that they had come off the trail only five minutes before us, and that they were about to look for a campsite for the night. When I mentioned that we still had another mile to walk to our cabins, I definitely had an ulterior motive. The girls offered to drop us off at our cabins, for which we were grateful.

Several weeks have passed since I conquered the summit of Mt. Whitney in one day. I have had time to reflect on the wonderful vistas and to evaluate this whole deep and satisfying experience. I have often been asked the question: would you do it again? My answer is definitely in the affirmative, for I know now that each time I climb the highest peak in the "lower 48" it will be a thrilling and spiritually rewarding journey. I began with the thought of doing it once in my lifetime—of achieving it being a this-year-or-never-proposition. I know now that climbing Mt. Whitney is too wonderful to remain just a one-time event in my memory. I want to do it again, because I know that each trip will offer different sights, new experiences, and a chance for me to feel once again the awesome power that comes with being on top of the world.

[*Note: Contains original spelling to preserve historical accuracy.*]

APPENDIX B

THE HIGHEST HOUSE IN AMERICA:
HOW THE NEW OBSERVATORY ON MT. WHITNEY WAS CONSTRUCTED
San Francisco Chronicle, Sunday, November 7, 1909
by
Harold French

Cemented to a granite foundation, 14,501 feet above sea level, a class A, fire and earthquake proof structure of stone and steel now crowns the crest of Mount Whitney, the highest point in the United States. The observatory was constructed late last August by the Smithsonian Institution, represented by Dr. Abbot, director of the Mount Wilson observatory, with the co-operation of Professor Alexander G. MacAdie of the United States Weather Bureau and Dr. Campbell, director of Lick Observatory. Concerning it, the latter of these noted men of science says: It is a great credit to the Smithsonian Institution and to the superintendent of the construction, G. F. Marsh, a public-spirited citizen of Lone Pine, who struggled, valiantly and successfully against the difficulties of transporting cement and steel to the summit, as well as difficulties of less open character. Marsh's connection with the project is one in which he is entitled to feel the utmost pride, and I trust that his fellow citizens of Lone Pine and Inyo County will appreciate his services in this connection.

Important as is the scientific value of this unique observatory, its deeper human interest lies in the heroic efforts of the men who blazed the trail. Indeed, the building of this citadel of science might have been indefinitely deferred were it not for the perseverance of a man with a high ideal. For eight long, discouraging years his fixed purpose of life was to accomplish the erection of an observatory on the summit of Mount Whitney, having the faith and foresight to realize what a great advantage such an attraction would be to his community, for whose betterment he labored. With a few resolute companions, he struggled with the elements far up that savage Sierran scarp, and by his force of character overcame the more insidious obstacles of jealousy and doubt which beset his path below. How these men of tried steel hewed their way through barriers of granite and ice, is a story for the pen of a Kipling to relate. Readers of realistic fiction who have reveled in The Bridge Builders or Caleb West, Master Diver, would find the facts regarding the building of the Lone Pine trail and the dream of the observatory fulfilled a volume of even more tensely thrilling interest.

PEOPLE OF LONE PINE PAVE WAY.

An eagle soaring from the summit of Mount Whitney toward the sunrise fourteen miles in an air line would glance nearly eleven thousand feet directly down upon the little town of Lone Pine. For more than a third of a century it has slumbered peacefully in the secluded valley of the Owens River, which skirts the eastern foothills of the Sierra for 100 miles down to the dead sea of California, Owens Lake. Then new blood revived these isolated towns of Inyo, and, following certain enterprising newcomers, came a railroad which will soon carry out the produce of Owens Valley. Twenty streams pouring forth from the Sierran snowfields are now being harnessed for the generation of more than 100,000 horse-power, while the water is being diverted to the rich valley soil with a degree of success that is repeating the history of irrigation in Southern California. Among these desirable citizens came an Englishman, Gustave F. Marsh, who, after investigating the opportunities of other districts of the awakening West, decided to share in the development of Inyo County.

He located in Lone Pine, and eight years ago joined with other progressive residents of Inyo County in agitating a popular sentiment in favor of building a pack trail to the summit of the mountain. With few exceptions the people of Lone Pine perceived that the construction of a safe trail up Mount Whitney would attract scientists to the summit, and that their influence might induce the Government to establish an observatory there, which would naturally bring their town into prominence. In August, 1903, Messrs. Spears, Cross and Spears, together with the photographer, Harvey, returned from a reconnoitering trip over the proposed route. Their reports were so favorable that the sum of $700 was promptly subscribed for the purpose of outfitting a party of fourteen, who, under the direction of Mr. Spears, constructed the trail up through the foaming canyon of Lone Pine creek, past the picturesque Lake of the Lonesome Pine to the pass of the same romantic name at an elevation of 13,000 feet. Although within three and one-half miles of the summit, the pioneer party was compelled to abandon the work because the funds had become exhausted.

The heroic and herculean task of carving a course, through granite ice and avalanche-accumulating slide rock was far more difficult and expensive than bargained for, and all who have struggled with the overwhelming forces of nature under similar circumstances will appreciate the disappointment of these men, who returned only when their supplies gave out.

It was at this juncture that the people of Inyo Couty rallied to the support of the project, and the Supervisors appropriated the sum of $200 to enable the trail builders to complete their work. Marsh was chosen to lead the second party, and although late in the season he started up with fifteen men, of whom seven deserted during the first few days. It was late in October, and at an elevation of two miles and a half the wind was bitterly cold, as it surged savagely around the dizzy cliffs. Sleet and icy rain beat down upon them, while avalanches would repeatedly obliterate their new-made trail. The sliding talus was treacherous, and when the men would blast a bowlder out of their path they would see, to their dismay, tons of rough angular rocks roll down into their path. It was heartbreaking work lifting these heavy masses, thousands and thousands of them, when the rarefied air of this high altitude made physical effort most fatiguing.

Although the thin atmosphere produced violent headaches and afflicted them with nausea, they nevertheless toiled on and upward. A huge barrier of ice and snow they bridged by throwing dirt and gravel upon its surface and packing it down until animals could pass over it in safety. In places it was necessary to blast through jutting ledges and the overhanging ramparts rang with the roar of the detonating dynamite. They buttressed the downward side of the trail with dovetailing bowlders of granite and lava and crammed the crevices with fragments of rubble until the footing was secure for the pack-laden horses and mules. Finally, on October 30th a blinding snowstorm proved the last straw. All day long they toiled with dogged desperation, despite the fact that they could barely distinguish one another, so thick and fast fell the flakes. After a long and bitter night, exposed to the fury of the storm, without a tent for shelter, they realized that they would be snowed in hopelessly if they lingered, and with the dawn they cached their tools and returned to Lone Pine, bitterly disappointed, but not discouraged.

"ONCE MORE UNTO THE BREACH."
Winter descended with all its rigors upon Mount Whitney, but the builders of the trail were far from hibernating down in the pleasant valley of the Owens. Three hundred dollars were required to complete the trail and the ladies of Lone Pine came to the front with the tidy sum of $69 netted from a basket social and dance, while the neighboring towns of Independence and Keeler contributed the generous sums of $85 and $67 respectively. Other residents of Inyo swelled the fund with hard-earned coin at considerable personal sacrifice in some cases, while many proffered their labor for a number of days for the common good of their county.

On July 8, 1904, the third expedition went to the front in the best of spirits and with the determination to win. Its members found the trail in excellent condition until they reached Mexican Camp, their base of supplies, 12,000 feet above the sea. Here their troubles began, and their animals broke through the snow. It became necessary to shovel a trench for 300 yards through the deep drift until they could lead the animals up to Lone Pine pass. In many places they were obliged to carry the packs on their own backs in order to encourage the skeptical and pessimistic mules. Firewood was carried up to a new camp at the elevation of 13,552 feet. From this point upward for the remaining thousand feet the men vied with one another to complete their allotted strips first. In the van proceeded the drillers, who blasted their way round hitherto impassable cliffs. When within but a few hundred yards of the summit they came upon a chasm which it seemed no human foot could cross. "We're done beat now for sure," the men groaned when they beheld the precipitous cliff, but Marsh only smiled and set the dynamite to work reducing the angle of the cliff until the gap was bridged with debris. At last, on the 17th of July, the builders of the trail had finished their work, and with a cheer the first pack train trampled the flat roof of Whitney. The packs consisted of pitch pine, rockets, and dynamite, and that night the watchers down in Lone Pine saw their beloved mountain transformed into a volcano, as the signal fire flamed from its crest and the salvos of dynamite rumbled down the gorges.

THEN THE OBSERVATORY.

For four years the trail served the worthy purpose of attracting increasing numbers of mountain lovers to Lone Pine. They ascended its scenic and sinuous curves past roaring cataracts to the placid Lone Pine and Mirror lakes, where gamy trout abide and abound. Government scientists scaled the summit from its now most accessible side, and determined its exact elevation to be 14,501 feet. In the summer of 1908 Mr. Marsh took Professors Abbot and Campbell, directors of the Mount Wilson and Lick observatories respectively, up to the summit of Mount Whitney on a tour of investigation. They were strongly impressed with the flat roof of the mountain as a splendid site for an observatory, and found the conditions of dry and clear atmosphere most favorable to important research work. In 1881 Professor Langley, the father of the aeroplane, camped for a number of weeks 3000 feet below the summit, conducting a series of experiments which enabled him to calculate the solar constant, or the total amount of heat the earth would receive from the sun if the atmosphere did not absorb a large percentage of its radiant energy.

Fifteen years ago Dr. Campbell had visited Mount Whitney and, realizing that its crest was above four-fifths of the moisture in the earth's atmosphere, he foresaw the value to science of a series of spectrographic photographs, which would determine the amount of water vapor in the atmosphere of our neighbor planets, particularly Mars. During all these years he warmly indorsed the project of establishing a shelter on this mountain top, where scientists may place their delicate apparatus and study the unsolved problems of astronomy, astro-physics, meteorology, biology and other kindred subjects. Now that the public-spirited people of Lone Pine had demonstrated the practicability of transporting building materials, supplies of all kinds and even the most delicate instruments with comparative safety to this lofty look-out ledge, the way was paved for the planning of the observatory that would crown their efforts with success. Dr. Abbot, representing the Smithsonian Institution, informed Mr. Marsh that a fund would be appropriated for this purpose if he would assure the officials in Washington that the trail would be put in first-class condition. Mr. Marsh agreed to his part, and secured, as the lowest bidder, the contract for packing some fourteen tons of cement, sand, steel, glass and other supplies to the summit during the ensuing summer.

BUILDING THE OBSERVATORY.

Five winters had wrapped white blankets around the frost-sculptured form of Whitney. Avalanches and storms had played ninepins with the trail, and once more the call for contributions came to the good people of Lone Pine and its altruistic neighbors. Again the ladies of Lone Pine came to the front with their choicest cakes, pies and other toothsome temptations. They served a savory supper after a merry dance, a happy combination which proved the event of the season. The population of Lone Pine is but 350, yet they cleared $130 that evening by charging the moderate rate of $1.50 a couple. The lemonade stand proved a bonanza, for its clean-up was just $13.90, while Independence and Keeler once more added their quota.

On the 18th of last July Marsh attacked the snow drifts above the timber line with a force of men, who with axes and grubbing-hoes hewed a path for the pack train to follow. For two days following the party was crippled with snow blindness, the torture of which is most excruciating; yet with masks made from gunny saks the men still labored on until the arrival of colored glasses relieved their torment. At 13,550 feet they were obliged to build a quarter of a mile of new trail in order to wind around a field of soft snow, while the work of reconstructing the old way required the frequent use of dynamite. Blinding headaches, extreme exhaustion resulting from hard manual labor in such rarefied air, all these were their daily portion. Once more the funds gave out and an increasing demand for labor down in the valley lured some of the men from the heights. A few, however, remained with Marsh to the last, when, on the 28th of July, the nimble-footed mules finally stood silhouetted against the indigo sky that hangs seemingly close to the summit.

As soon as the long-eared collaborators were relieved of their burdens, the foundation was commenced. A camp was established in a sheltered cranny where a supply of firewood accumulated. Snow was melted on pieces of sheetiron roofing and the water used to mix with cement. Walls of re-enforced concrete rose rapidly upward. Then came a terrifying thunderstorm, and Marsh was deserted by the last of his men. Alone on the summit he set his teeth and with unflinching grit decided to complete the observatory single handed, but after two days his helpers returned and finished their work. On the 29th of last August, this pioneer building was ready to serve its purpose as a shelter for scientific expeditions. It is thirty feet in length, twelve in width and ten in height, and is divided into three rooms, one of which will remain unlocked as "a shelter in the time of storm" for the accommodation of tourists. It is hoped that this favor will be appreciated by all who may seek refuge in this life-saving station on the peak, where decades ago John Muir danced all night to keep from freezing.

An expedition from Lick Observatory was financed last August by a Regent of the University of California, and Dr. W. W. Campbell was chosen to lead the party, which consisted of several from Mount Hamilton, Dr. Miller of San Jose and Professor MacAdie of the Weather Bureau. The party left Lone Pine on August 28th, and after spending two days at Lone Pine lake in order to become acclimated to the altitude, they joined Dr. Abbot, the director of the Smithsonian Institution Observatory, whom they found engaged in a remarkably thorough study of the intensity of the solar radiation.

Dr. Campbell transported a sixteen-inch horizontal-reflecting telescope with spectroscopic attachments, with which he made certain discoveries of great astronomical importance. He demonstrated the absence of water vapor in appreciable quantities in the atmosphere of Mars by means of photographing its spectrum. Had water been present to the slightest extent, the solar rays passing through the atmosphere of Mars and being reflected to the earth would have shown a distant dark band on the photographic plate. Only the faintest vapor band was revealed by the spectroscope in the analysis of the light rays traversing the Martian atmosphere, and even this could be attributed to the small percentage of moisture in the atmosphere of our earth still suspended above the summit of Whitney. The result of this discovery would tend to refute the canal theory of Schiaparelli and those of the yellow journal scientific contributors, who still maintain that life, such as we know, exists in a waterless atmosphere.

FUTURE SCOPE OF OBSERVATORY.

Professor MacAdie, the meteorologist who accompanied the Campbell party, was one of the first and most ardent advocates of Mount Whitney as an observatory site, because of its accessibility, clear sky and its elevation above the water vapor of lower levels. On his recent visit he spent seven nights on the summit where he studied the phenomena of the upper air from a most favorable vantage point. As a meteorological station where the laws of storms may be studied and the changes of temperature and barometric pressure may be better understood, Mount Whitney will add greatly to the knowledge of a devoted corps of Government scientists who desire to apply the facts they will learn to the daily needs of the farmer folk down in the valleys below. The observatory will doubtless attract the more progressive men of science who will take advantage of its opportunities for research work along the lines of their respective specialties, and in the course of the next few years it will probably be enlarged to accommodate the pilgrims to this mountain-Mecca.

WHAT WHITNEY OVERLOOKS.

One can never imagine the majesty of this mountain until he sees with his own eyes the grandeur of the sunrise. Six thousand feet sheer, the titanic fault scarp falls away to the dun and drab foothills at its base. Grotesque pinnacles and the eerie and weirdly-carved crags burn red above the spotless whiteness of the snowfields. Below for a hundred miles the Owens' valley drains into its saline sea. Its floor, however, is a green oasis, where the magic touch of water is transforming 1000 square miles of grazing land into highly productive orchards and vineyards. The raisin grape is becoming a popular favorite among these ranchers of Inyo, whose dry climate guarantees the successful curing of the sugary crop. Half-way up the savage saw-toothed slopes the eagle soars over forests of fox-tail pine and shaggy tamaracks, and sees his image reflected in countless crystal lakes whose foaming outlets are ordained to turn the wheels of future industries.

Beyond the green gladness of the Owens vale, the mineralized Inyo mountains swell, and over them still the painted Panamints pierce the sky over toward the great mysterious desert, where stretch the sunken sandy wastes of Death Valley seventy fathoms below the level of Balboa's sea.

[*edited version, with some original spelling & punctuation*]

APPENDIX C

LETTER TO W. W. CAMPBELL DESCRIBING OBSERVATIONS OF HALLEY'S COMET FROM THE SUMMIT OF MOUNT WHITNEY

June 5, 1910
by
Gustave F. Marsh

Lone Pine, California   5 June 1910

Prof W. W. Campbell, Mt. Hamilton

Dear Sir,

Your kind letter to hand Friday night.... (answering your inquiry about my observations of Halley's Comet from the summit of Mt. Whitney last May.) I was very anxious to see the building & so many promised to go with me but they all fell down at the last minute. So I determined to go alone for J. E. Church kindly loaned me snowshoes. So I started Sunday morning 8:30 & figured to be on the top at 12 AM next day & see the Comet & Eclipse. I drove to the power plant & started to walk at 12 AM. I took 1 Blanket, 1 piece of Canvas, some tea & coffee, 1 can Baked bean, snow shoes & 1/2 pint whiskey. It made quite a load. I took my time & got to Lone Pine Lake 4:20 & Robinson's Camp at 5 PM. First snow at 10000 ft., trail all good so far with small patches of snow off and on to timber line.

I fixed my camp, built a big fire, gathered up all the old sacks I could find & old clothes & made me a pretty good bed with some boxes for a wind break. I passed the night very comfortable. I got up at 3 AM, ate my breakfast & started out just as it was light enough, about 4 AM. The Snow was just right for traveling. No frost at Robinson's Camp. I made good time to that first big snow bank. There the snow was so hard I could not get a footing. My snow shoes would not hold so I took to the rocks & with my snow shoes & pack it was quite a task, but I did fine. It was good going till I got to about 12,500 about where the ice was last year. There I found the snow very hard and smooth, that was about 6 AM.

I could not use my snow shoes, so I used them to dig holes for my feet. I found that was very difficult, I needed an alpine stock then. I had to stamp my feet down till I got a footing & the higher I got the worse it got & I dare not turn round, so I made a bee line for the cliffs towards the east but oh my it was so slow. I had to make sure of every step, but I made it in safety. At Lone Pine side I never saw the snow so smooth & hard & it was easy going to Lake View Camp. From there, there was very little snow till I got to the big bank near Mt. Whitney, but it was easy going. I got to the top at 11:15 oh but I was tired.

I made a fire & started my can of beans for soup. Took out the mirror & at 12 noon I signaled to Lone Pine & got an answer in 3 minutes. I had promised my wife I would signal at 12. After I got an answer I felt pretty good. I ate my bean soup, sat out in the sun, looked around & saw a big fat ground Hog sitting by the monument. He did not seem a bit afraid, he came & packed off some old bread I had thrown out.

I found the building in good shape, only the door to the room for the tourist was down & the room was half full of snow & it's pretty sure someone did not fasten it very well or left it open entirely. It can be put back in a few minutes with help. Quite a bit of snow had drifted in the other two rooms through the door ventilators & laps in the roof. I find it will be necessary to close up every crevice.

There was no snow on top of the mountain. It was a beautiful day & I got ready to see the comet, but at 5 PM it got cloudy, but the moon came up full speed alright & was clear as a bell, but towards night it clouded again & for the first quarter of the moon it was cloudy, but after that it was clear.

The comet was in plain view as soon as it was dark & just before the moon was covered the sky was perfectly clear except the fog bank very low down towards Visalia & the comet showed up grand & was in plane sight until the head of the comet got in the fog bank it seemed particularly bright at about 8:30 when the moon was almost covered the tail almost reached the moon, it swept almost across the sky.

I slept good. I had quite a headache at times. I made a signal fire at night & saw 5 fires in return. The minimum temperature was 23 degrees below zero & max 55 (as recorded by McAdie's thermometers left there last September). There was 10% frost the night of the 23rd. At 5 PM it was 36 & at 7 AM it was 22. I left the top at 7 AM & got home in town at 2:30. I found it more difficult coming down the snow on the Lone Pine side than it was going up, but I kept on the rocks all I could. I slipped once but did not slide very far.

I was very tired for days. Hoping to see you again soon. I shall be glad to introduce you to Maule Whitney Marsh born March 21st.

Best Love to all from us all

Yours Truly,

G. F. Marsh

APPENDIX D

LISTS OF FLOWERS AND BIRDS SEEN FROM WHITNEY PORTAL TO TULAINYO LAKE OVERLOOK
by Marcyn Del Clements
March, 2002

Introduction to Lists:
When Doug Thompson from the Portal Store led me up the Mountaineer's route in June 2000, into the Carillon mesas (called for the prominent peak to the west) and up to the overlook of Tulainyo Lake, I was exhausted but awestruck. Not only was this fishless lake starkly beautiful, at 12,802 feet a.s.l., but hardly anyone ever came here, especially not by the way we climbed, up through the mesas.

I was so enchanted by this place and the thought that Indians had been here and stayed, that I made a second pilgrimage all alone a month later.

Doug and I were interested in what was blooming. Being an amateur naturalist, I always want to name things and look things up. He encouraged me to make a list.

It was interesting to me that when we hiked up in June, it was full summer for the flowers, but when I climbed up barely over a month later, in August, it was already turning fall in the high country, with the Rabbitbrush blooming and many more flowers in the Sunflower Family.

I'd like to mention that this entire route is not for the faint of heart! But if you go there, following Doug's instructions, you too may feel the presence of ancient peoples before you; you too may feel the enchantment.

-Marcyn Del Clements, 1 March 2002

A LIST OF FLOWERS SEEN FROM WHITNEY PORTAL TO TULAINYO LAKE OVERLOOK
as seen on June 27-28, 2000
(possible & probable)

Compiled by Marcyn Del Clements, with research assistance from husband, Richard F. Clements.

Order presented is based on the field guide: *Sierra Nevada Wildflowers* by Elizabeth L. Horn.

BUCKWHEAT FAMILY
- *Eriogonum species*, poss. *nudum* (dry slopes)
- *Oxyria digyna*, Mountain Sorrel (sheltering next to rocks)

BUTTERCUP FAMILY
- *Aquilegia formosa*, Crimson Columbine (Flower Garden, named by Doug Thompson—a mesic area below the Carillon outfall)

CARROT FAMILY
- *Heracleum lanatum*, Cow Parsnip (in Fern Wood, also called Cedar Grove, at very beginning above main Mt. Whitney Trail)
- *Sphenosciadium capitellum*, Ranger's Buttons (Flower Garden)

EVENING PRIMROSE FAMILY
- *Epilobium angustifolium*, Fireweed (Flower Garden & elsewhere)
- *Castilleja species*, poss. *miniata*, Indian Paintbrush (mesic areas)

FIGWORT FAMILY
- *Penstemon davidsonii*, Davidson's Penstemon (dry slopes) *Penstemon rydbergii*, Meadow Penstemon

GENTIAN FAMILY
- *Gentianopsis holopetala*, Sierra Fringed Gentian (Flower Garden)

GOOSEBERRY FAMILY
- *Ribes species*, both Currant and Gooseberry. (Gooseberries have spines, Currants do not.) (along the slopes)

HEATH FAMILY
- *Ledum glandulosum*, Labrador Tea
- *Phyllodoce breweri*, Red Heather (esp. in ravine near Indian Camp)
- *Sarcodes sanguinea*, Snow Plant (very beginning, Fern Wood)

IRIS FAMILY
- *Sisyrinchium bellum*, Blue-Eyed Grass

LEGUME FAMILY
- *Lupinus species*, Lupine

OAK FAMILY
- *Chrysolepis sempervirens*, Bush Chinquapin (ubiquitous)

PHLOX FAMILY
- *Ipomopsis aggregata*, Scarlet Gilia
- *Polemonium eximium*, Sky Pilot (only end of route, above mesas)

PRIMROSE FAMILY
- *Dodecatheon jeffreyi*, Jeffrey Shooting Star
- *Primula suffrutescens*, Sierra Primrose (up high, on way to overlook)

PURSLANE FAMILY
- *Calyptridium umbellatum*, Pussypaws
- *Claytonia perfoliata*, Miner's Lettuce (first stream crossing)

ROSE FAMILY
- *Cercocarpus ledifolius*, Curl-Leaf Mountain Mahogany *Chamaebatia foliolosa*, Mountain Misery
- *Rosa woodsii*, Wood's Rose (Flower Garden)

STONECROP FAMILY
- *Sedum rosea*, Western Roseroot, or Rosy Sedum (higher up, cliff-side)

SUNFLOWER FAMILY
- *Aster alpigenus*, Alpine Aster
- *Erigeron species*, prob. *pygmaeus*, Dwarf Daisy
- *Hulsea algida*, Alpine Gold or Alpine Hulsea (at overlook to Tulainyo)

VIOLET FAMILY
- *Viola adunca*, Western Long-spurred Violet

Added to list (or confirmed) from Solo trip on August 14-15, 2000 (From Portal to "Indian Encampment" only). Also reflects not only new insights, but changes in what is now blooming, over what was blooming a month ago.—MDC

BUCKWHEAT FAMILY
- *Eriogonum nudum*, Nude Buckwheat (for sure, especially up on Carillon mesas in the dry slopes)

BUTTERCUP FAMILY
- *Actaea rubra*, Baneberry (at first stream crossing & again in mesic area above Lower Boy Scout Lake)

EVENING PRIMROSE FAMILY
- *Epilobium canum*, California Fuchsia (along dry slopes, especially on the overhanging seep north of Lower Boy Scout Lake)
- *Castilleja applegatei*, Applegate Paintbrush (on dry slopes) *Castilleja miniata*, Indian Paintbrush (in the meadows)

FIGWORT FAMILY
- *Mimulus guttatus*, (Slimy-leaved) Monkeyflower (at overhang seep)
- *Penstemon rostriflorus*, Bridge's Penstemon (Flower Garden)

LEGUME FAMILY
- *Lupinus latifolius*, Broad-leaved Lupine (Flower Garden)

MINT FAMILY
- *Stachys albens*, White Hedgenettle (Fern Woods a.k.a. Cedar Grove)

ROSE FAMILY
- *Ivesia santolinoides*, Mousetails (all over Indian Camp area on mesas, a miniscule flower but with furry soft leaves)

SAXIFRAGE FAMILY
- *Heuchera rubescens*, Alumroot (Carillon mesas, sheltered in rocks)

SUNFLOWER FAMILY
- *Achillea millefolium*, Yarrow (dry slopes)
- *Chrysothamnus nauseosus*, Rubber Rabbitbrush (late bloomer) [possibly Ericameria too, but I didn't distinguish them—that's the trouble with being an amateur]
- *Helenium bigelovii*, Bigelow Sneezeweed (Flower Garden, and an interesting dwarf form at the streamside on the mesas. Are they the same?)
- *Senecio triangularis*, Arrowleaf Butterweed (Indian Camp, streamside)

- *Solidago multiradiata*, Alpine Goldenrod (same place, growing along stream in that meadow on the Carillon Mesa)

Note on trees: both Whitebark Pine (*Pinus albicaulis*) and Foxtail Pine (*Pinus balfouriana*) were present at my Indian Camp on the Carillon Mesa. I found the small cones with incurved prickles and a slightly larger, purple cone, with no prickles. They both have 5 needles and exhibit the slight Krumholz effect of wind. But on the mesa, I think the Whitebark pines were taller, straighter.

Shooting Star below Iceberg Lake

A LIST OF BIRDS HEARD OR SEEN FROM WHITNEY PORTAL TO TULAINYO LAKE OVERLOOK
on June 27-28, 2000
(in approximate phylogenetic order)

- American Kestrel
- Blue Grouse
- Mountain Quail
- Rufous Hummingbird (a migrant)
- Northern Flicker
- Red-naped Sapsucker
- Steller's Jay
- Clark's Nutcracker
- Common Raven
- Mountain Chickadee
- White-breasted Nuthatch
- American Dipper
- Swainson's Thrush
- American Robin
- Townsend's Solitaire
- American Pipit
- Yellow-rumped Warbler
- Dark-eye Junco
- Grey-crowned Rosy-Finch
- Cassin's Finch
- Golden-crowned Kinglet (October 3, 2000)

Even in mid-winter—with nary an unguarded French fry in sight—you'll find the ubiquitous Steller's Jay keeping an expectant eye on the Portal Store...

APPENDICES

APPENDIX E

CONGRESSIONAL RECORD
OF THE
UNITED STATES OF AMERICA

<u>VOL. 144, NO. 143</u>
<u>WASHINGTON, MONDAY, OCTOBER 12, 1998</u>

House of Representatives

CELEBRATING THE RICH HISTORY OF MT. WHITNEY

HON. JERRY LEWIS
OF CALIFORNIA
IN THE HOUSE OF REPRESENTATIVES
Monday, October 12, 1998

Mr. Speaker, I would like to bring to your attention today the 125th anniversary of the first ascent of Mt. Whitney, the highest mountain peak in the continental United States at 14,494 feet, located in California's Inyo County.

In the early 1870's, as the Owens Valley community first began to attract settlers, local residents often visited nearby Soda Springs to fish, hunt, and to escape the summer heat. In August of 1873, a large group of Lone Pine locals were camping in this area when three of them decided to take a hike up to the summit. Previous attempts to climb this mountain had been made by Clarence King, in party with a California Geological Survey expedition sponsored by Josiah Whitney. King identified the mountain and named it "Mount Whitney" in 1864. He claimed to have reached the summit in 1871, but it was soon discovered that he missed the mark and accidentally climbed another peak.

The "Three Fishermen" (locals Charley Begole, Johnny Lucas and Al Johnson) credited with Whitney's first ascent made the hike from Soda Springs to the summit and back in one day on August 18, 1873. They christened the mountain "Fishermen's Peak," which touched off a controversy that lasted several years. The Lone Pine residents were not in favor of the name "Mount Whitney," since they did not share a high opinion of Mr. Whitney. Local residents petitioned in favor of the names "Fishermen's Peak," "Fowler's Peak," or "Dome of Inyo," anything but "Mount Whitney," which is the name that stands today.

Undaunted by the unwanted name, local residents raised funds and built a trail to the summit in 1904. Mr. Gustave F. Marsh of Lone Pine was the engineer who led this effort. He also served as contractor and supervisor for the Smithsonian Institute in 1909 when the trail was repaired and the summit shelter was built. Local residents again pitched in to raise funds for this effort. The summit hut was originally financed by the Smithsonian for astronomical and atmospheric research purposes.

The early residents of the region were largely farmers and miners. As the trail and hut stand today, no one really knows how many hundreds of thousands of people from all walks of life and from all countries of the world have climbed to the summit of Mount Whitney. Also, very little has ever been mentioned of the Native Americans, who knew of the peak and in their world, called it "The Old One," or "The High One."

On August 18, 1998, as a tribute to these early settlers, another group of local residents climbed Mount Whitney to pay honor to the contribution made by these pioneers. Several descendants of the original group still live in the Lone Pine area.

I can well remember donning a backpack and sleeping bag and hitting the trail with Hulda Crooks, better known on the mountain as Grandma Whitney, in August, 1986. A friendship was born over those days that has been among the most special and enduring of my life. Because of her legacy, Congress passed legislation and Hulda returned to Mt. Whitney in 1991 for the announcement that Crooks Peak, adjacent to the Whitney summit, would forever bear her name. Hulda was a mentor and teacher and

remained one of my dearest friends over the years until her passing last November.

Mr. Speaker, I ask that you join me and our colleagues in paying tribute to the men and women who have provided Mt. Whitney with its rich and textured history. Without any question, for every person who has ever climbed or tried to climb this magnificent peak, Mt. Whitney holds its own special memories, and its own meaningful place in their life.

[*Note: Timeline "__ years ago" based on original 1999 publication date.*]

APPENDIX F

TIMELESS MOUNTAIN
by
Elisabeth Newbold and Doug Thompson
Published in a special Millennium Edition
of the
Inyo Register
November 25, 1999

"...escape to the mountain, lest thou be consumed."
(Genesis 19:17)

We stand before the mileage sign of the New Millennium, pondering time and how it changes things. The past 1,000 years have engraved dramatic alterations upon many features of our planet. Some, however, stand impervious.

Today, "web cams" broadcast rapidly changing images of weather, waves, and landscapes worldwide. But if we had an archive containing clips of Mount Whitney shot every month for the past 1,000 years (a total of 12,000 shots) the changes would barely be perceptible.

If greatly enlarged, the last 150 frames might reveal evidence of humans on the horizon: a trail in the making, a hut on the summit, bonfires signaling visits to the top. Let's focus in, and sift through the last 100-plus years of events at Mount Whitney:

- First Ascent: August 18, 1873, 126 years ago. It was a group of three men who first stood on the summit—fishing buddies from Lone Pine. Previous attempts by Clarence King had failed. Charley Begole, Johnny Lucas, and Al Johnson carved their names in history one summer day, when they climbed the mountain on an impulse. Locals dubbed it "Fisherman's

Peak," but the official name became "Mount Whitney," named after Josiah Whitney, Professor at the California Academy of Sciences and founder of the California Geological Survey.

- First Overnight Stay on Top: September 2-3, 1881, 118 years ago. Summer was drawing to a close when Captain Otho E. Michaelis, along with two or three others of his party, hauled a tent and a quarter-cord of wood to the top. The wind was so fierce they could not put up the tent, and their campfire consumed all of their wood long before the sun came up. Like many others since, they did not get any sleep during their cold night on the summit of Mount Whitney.

- Completion of Mt. Whitney Trail: July 17, 1904, 95 years ago. The trail was begun in 1903, but efforts fizzled as supplies ran out. The people of Inyo County rallied to support the project, raised $200, and contracted Gustave F. Marsh to take over the effort. Enduring cold, wind, and snow until the end of October, Marsh and his small crew were disappointed to leave the trail unfinished. During the winter, fund-raising activities yielded enough to support renewed efforts the following season. From "The Highest House" printed in the *San Francisco Chronicle*, Sunday, Nov. 7, 1909:
    > "When within but a few hundred yards of the summit they came upon a chasm which it seemed no human foot could cross. 'We're done beat now for sure,' the men groaned when they behold the precipitous cliff, but Marsh only smiled and set the dynamite to work reducing the angle of the cliff until the gap was bridged with debris. At last, on the 17th of July, the builders of the trail had finished their work and with a cheer the first pack train trampled the flat roof of Whitney."

- Completion of Summit Shelter: August 27, 1909, 90 years ago. The Smithsonian Institution contracted Mr. Marsh to build the summit shelter. The trail needed repair before this could be accomplished. Marsh and his crew suffered snow blindness, altitude sickness, and limited resources. It took until July 28 to reestablish the trail and lead the first pack train to the summit. Work quickly commenced on the stone hut. As it took shape, a violent thunderstorm drove all but Marsh into desertion. He resolved to finish the hut if he had to do it by himself. Thanks to his tenacity, the others returned a few days later. The shelter was completed two days early, and $250 under budget. Dr. Charles Abbot, Director of the Smithsonian Astrophysical Observatory, wrote that Marsh "will never get paid in this world for the work he did on that house," which included cooking, carrying stone and snow, riveting and cementing, as well as "general bossing."

- Visit of Halley's comet: May 23, 1910, 89 years ago. Again we turn to Gustave Marsh for another "freeze frame" in Mount Whitney's recent history. Marsh climbed the peak alone to watch the sky show: a total lunar eclipse plus the comet. "...The moon came up full speed ... for the first quarter of the moon it was cloudy but after that it was clear. The comet was in plain view as soon as it was dark ... [it] showed up grand and was in plain sight until the head ... got in the fog bank. It seemed particularly bright at about 8:30 ... when the moon was almost covered. The tail almost reached the moon. It swept almost across the sky. I feel I had the best view of anyone outside of an observatory." (G. F. Marsh, Letter to Prof. W. W. Campbell, June 5, 1910)

- First Airplane Flight over Whitney Summit: 1914, 85 years ago. Residents of Inyo, Mono and Alpine counties joined together to promote attention to the Owens Valley. The Inyo Good Road Club organized and publicized this event, which took place during Aviation Week. Silas Christofferson flew a tractor biplane over the Whitney summit on the morning of June 25, setting a new altitude record for flight: 15,725 feet. Powered by a 100 HP engine, the plane weighed a total of 1,850 pounds, including the pilot, one passenger, and 30 gallons of gas.

- Construction of Road, Pond, Campgrounds: 1933-35, 64 years ago. As more people came to visit Mount Whitney, more accommodations were built. The original Whitney Portal Road was constructed in 1933-35, making it possible for tourists to drive their automobiles up from Lone Pine into the lush little canyon. The original route followed the early pack trail, and a small part of it can be seen today below the existing road, an area known in the past as "Hunter's Flat." Public campgrounds, picnic areas, and a fishing pond were built by the post-depression Civilian Conservation Corps (CCC), with the U.S. Forest Service, to enhance the region. The Forest Service maintained the public areas until recently, when some services were subcontracted out. Most visitors are not aware of the work behind the scenes. It is the time and effort of both paid employees and volunteers that keep the road clear, the trees healthy, the bathrooms clean, and the trash removed.

- "Wedding of the Waters" Event: 1935, 64 years ago. Father John J. Crowley was much more to Inyo County than a Catholic priest. He adopted the entire community and was beloved by many people of all denominations. His vision included growth and prosperity for the area, and he used his flair for public relations to stage this press event. Indian runners filled a gourd with pure, icy water from the nation's highest lake (Lake Tulainyo) just north of Mount Whitney's summit. The gourd was transported in turn by pony express, burro, covered wagon, mule team, railroad car, and airplane. Finally, it was sprinkled from the plane into Badwater in Death Valley, the lowest body of water in the U.S. News of this fascinating ceremony spread all over California and beyond, focusing widespread attention on the region.

- Construction of Whitney Portal Store: 1935, 64 years ago. The Whitney Portal Store and pack station was built in 1935. It has changed hands several times, and it is hard to find a long-time local who hasn't cooked hamburgers at the Store or worked on pack trips.

- Construction of Cabins: 1935-1950, 50 years ago. The private cabin lots were each claimed and developed individually. These summer homes were built over a period of 16 years. Their varying sizes, styles, and decor attest to each one's unique design. One cabin burned down in 1950, and was rebuilt. Two more suffered serious damage in the great storms of 1969. That memorable winter was a harsh reminder of what nature can do when its full power is unleashed in the Eastern Sierra.

- Passage of Wilderness Act: 1964, 34 years ago. The heavy traffic through Whitney Portal and on the Whitney Trail took its toll. Concern about preserving the natural habitat led to adding the Whitney area to the Wilderness Act in 1964. This put strict limitations on the area—no mechanical equipment or new buildings, with very few exceptions.

- Ban of Pack Animals, Use of Trail Permits: 1970's, 25 years ago. In a continued effort to limit the impact of visitors on the Whitney Trail, the Forest Service banned pack animals in the 1970's. While horses, mules, and even llamas are still used in other areas of the back country for transporting equipment and supplies, they are no longer allowed on Mount Whitney. A quota system was put into place, requiring overnight permits.

- Regrowth of Outpost Camp, Mirror Lake: 1980's, 15 years ago. With pack animals no longer on the Whitney Trail, and foot traffic somewhat reduced by the quota system, meadows and other grassy areas had a chance to recover from overuse. The large, flat area now known as Outpost Camp (or Bighorn Sheep Park) had suffered from the annual trampling and grazing. The fragile section around Mirror Lake was also damaged. These areas experienced dramatic regrowth during the 1980's, and are once again lush with vegetation.

- Use of bear boxes, cell phones, web pages: 1990's, 5 years ago. One would expect that bear sightings might be less frequent than they were 100 years ago, but the Whitney Portal bears have adapted to the 1990's by losing their fear of man and developing a taste for junk food. Widespread damage to parked cars containing food has led to the installation of bear-proof containers at the Whitney Portal campgrounds. Other new developments include information access on the Internet, and the common use of digital/wireless telephones. Recently, a message was posted on the Whitney Portal Store's web site (mountwhitneyforum.com) by a hiker who observed he was the only one on the summit without a cell phone. In contrast, Gustave Marsh (in 1909) signaled his wife in Lone Pine with a mirror by day and a bonfire by night. Technology has exploded in the last decade, offering intriguing new toys for the backpacker. Instead of a compass and map, one can own a personal GPS (global positioning system). Instead of a journal, one can type the daily log into a palmtop computer.

Returning our focus to the wide angle lens, all this change is a mere pebble on the rocky granite buttresses that loom above us as we scan the horizon of Mount Whitney. When we stand back and think about it, nothing much about this landmark has really changed. A comfortable presence, it keeps its timeless watch over the surrounding peaks and valleys.

Those of us who are close neighbors of Mount Whitney need to remember its global significance. Thousands of visitors from all over the world have passed through Whitney Portal. The history of the mountain was important enough to elicit an entry in the U.S. Congressional Record last year.

The Mountain is still there. People still sense the need to climb it—to reach for something higher. However, what you may see nowadays, from the 360-degree view on the summit, is a degradation of air quality in all directions. Sometimes the Whitney drainage is so covered with dust from Owens Lake, you can't see the mountain. The frequent noise from low-flying aircraft distracts from the natural experience of hiking the trail. While Mount Whitney stands stalwart, the encroachments of nearby communities threaten its sanctity. As areas alongside of the wilderness develop, the impact tends to spill over. Thus, measures taken in neighboring cities—even several hundred miles away—may affect the quality of the Mount Whitney wilderness experience more than what is done locally. Perhaps this should be the focus of the next 100 years.